Praise for One Love

One Love offers a peek into the realm beyond and gives us the peace of knowing that our souls are connected even after life on earth. This was impactful, inspirational, and moving; a must read.

-Denice Choka, MBA
Director of Human Resources, Leanin' Tree

I thoroughly enjoyed reading Ruth's journey as she explored her recently discovered clairvoyant abilities and worked with archangels to heal lost souls. I found a new depth and understanding of my own spirituality through *One Love*, and a longing to learn even more!

-Kathy Silbert, LMT, NMT
Intuitive

One Love is a brave and nuanced body of writing, challenging the time-space continuum. It's perceptions and manifestation of spirit beings invite us to examine our constructs of life and death. Ruth's narrative is a courageous exploration of her spiritual journey; her memoir provides a very moving, inspirational reflection of her personal struggles and victories in the spiritual realm. Ruth generously shares her experiences and her gift of intuitive healing. She illustrates the depth of healing we can all access if we are open to it.

-Constance Frank, LCSW
Social Worker

Wow! *One Love* was a very captivating read! I didn't want to put it down; each story left me more and more intrigued and wanting to see where Ruth's journey would lead. I didn't want it to end! The experiences that Ruth described at Open Clinic were amazing. Her description of each story was so detailed, I could see them each clearly and felt the emotions in each one. The last chapter with the messages from the Divine Mother and the Archangels was fascinating and really spoke to me. Ruth is truly gifted: her wisdom and healing are extraordinary. Her book is amazing!

-Hillary Dunford
Intuitive

Many of our everyday actions and encounters are assumed to be merely unique coincidences or happenstance. *One Love* shows us this may not be the case. With keen insight, appreciated humor, unassuming questioning and admirable vulnerability, Anderson shares her clear and candid journey of spiritual understanding and transformation. In the process of honestly telling her story, readers are left with enlightening and inspiring lessons and aha's.

-Donna M. Sobel, Ph.D.
Assistant Director, Center for Faculty Development
University of Colorado Denver

ONE LOVE

ONE LOVE

Divine Healing at Open Clinic

A Personal Narrative By
Ruth Anderson

One Love: Divine Healing at Open Clinic
Published by SageHouse Press
Louisville, CO

Copyright ©2017 Ruth Anderson. All rights reserved.

No part of this book may be reproduced in any form or by any mechanical means, including information storage and retrieval systems without permission in writing from the publisher/author, except by a reviewer who may quote passages in a review.

All images, logos, quotes, and trademarks included in this book are subject to use according to trademark and copyright laws of the United States of America.

Library of Congress Control Number: 2016920430

Anderson, Ruth, Author
One Love: Divine Healing at Open Clinic
Ruth Anderson

ISBN: 978-0-9984573-0-7

BODY, MIND, SPIRIT / Healing/Prayer & Spiritual
BODY, MIND, SPIRIT / Angels & Spirit Guides

QUANTITY PURCHASES: Schools, companies, professional groups, clubs, and other organizations may qualify for special terms when ordering quantities of this title. For information, email SageHousePress@gmail.com

All rights reserved by Ruth Anderson and SageHouse Press
Book is printed in the United States of America.

This book is dedicated to my loving family.
I have often said that friends are chosen family.
If you were not my family,
I would choose you to be my friends.

And to my beautiful friend, Sylvia.
A lifetime was not long enough to love you.

Contents

Author's Note	11
Chapter 1: Diary of a Reluctant Psychic	13
Chapter 2: Sylvia	33
Chapter 3: Learning to See with New Eyes	45
Chapter 4: Back to School	61
Chapter 5: The Teacher	71
Chapter 6: Enter the Divine	83
Chapter 7: Animal Communication	93
Chapter 8: One Love	103
Chapter 9: Open Clinic	115
Chapter 10: Stories from Open Clinic	131
Chapter 11: Life Lessons in Open Clinic	149
Chapter 12: The Intrepid Traveler	157
Chapter 13: Journey of the Soul	177
Chapter 14: The Ministry on Earth	183
Chapter 15: From the Archangels	197

Author's Note

Why write a book? Because I was told to. This is probably an unusual way to introduce a book, but it's true. Do I always do what others tell me? No, but this chain of events is pretty unusual. The unusual thing is not that I learned to accept and embrace my intuition. The unusual thing is where this journey has led and where it might be heading.

    I am not an open book, which is humorous because here I am writing a book. I tend to keep my emotions and my innermost thoughts quite private. However, this story, these stories, need to be told. They need to be heard. I have been given these experiences and vignettes to share with others, so that they too can experience healing. My hope is that my journey can be instrumental or inspirational for your own journey.

My only disclaimer: I understand how outlandish this all may sound; one year ago I would have thought that too. In my classes and readings we have discussed spirit guides, healing masters, psychic surgeons, and nonhuman (alien) life-forms, so these encounters no longer seem strange to me. I have learned that I will never know everything there is to know about how this world works. The day I think I have it all figured out, I will know I am a fool for sure. I made a promise to narrate the things I have witnessed and learned, and I have tried to describe them chronologically, in enough detail so the reader can share in the experience. I am not an expert in any of these topics, except for my own experiences.

CHAPTER 1

Diary of a Reluctant Psychic

I can't tell you how many times I have heard that everyone has the ability to read energy; anyone can hone their sixth sense of intuition. But what if I just don't want to? Umm, no thanks!

DON'T GO IN THE BASEMENT

I grew up in the 1960s, the youngest child of two working parents. Being a latchkey child, I was home frequently by myself. I hated it. No matter how long I had to wait, when I was alone I sat at the kitchen table, seated in the one chair in which I could keep an eye on the TV and three doors at the same time: the door to the garage, the patio slider, and the door to the dreaded basement. I was always afraid.

I thought all kids grew up thinking their basements were haunted. In retrospect, I am not sure that is the case. I would venture down to the basement only if someone else was home; even then, I preferred that they were in the kitchen or already downstairs. Anytime I had to go down the stairs, I would stand at the top, flip on the lights and listen for noises downstairs. I never heard any, but that didn't dissuade me from checking. My heart racing, I would quickly run down the stairs, and jump past the open doorway to the right. This was the door that opened to my father's woodworking room, nicknamed The Shop. I would run straight to my desired location, grab what I needed, and run back up the stairs as fast as humanly possible, again avoiding the doorway to The Shop.

I determined that skipping any of the thirteen wooden steps would actually slow me down and throw me off balance if I needed to turn and defend myself. I didn't exhale until my feet landed safely back in the kitchen and I closed the basement door behind me. Not knowing what lurked in The Shop or what might grab me as I ran upstairs elicited a true fight or flight response. Every time. For the lack of actual experiences I had, my level of abject terror made no sense.

The Shop

My father enjoyed woodworking and had a room filled with tools and carpentry equipment. The unfinished space was perfect for leaving sawdust on the floor and storing half-completed projects. The Shop included a dirt crawlspace under the house that provided much needed storage for our family. No windows meant a pitch-dark room unless the fluorescent overhead lights were turned on. The light switch was inconveniently located so that a small child could not reach it. In place of a wooden door, my mother hung a brightly-striped orange piece of fabric from the ceiling, which served as a doorway to The Shop.

My father worked diligently at his career, leaving very little time for woodworking. Consequently, The Shop was rarely used. Months would go by with no one entering or turning on the light. I knew nothing about reading energy, but I knew The Shop was to be avoided.

I found out recently that my brother, who is two years older than I, was also insanely afraid of our basement. We commiserated as he explained his strategy for running the stairs and avoiding The Shop doorway. As he said, "You never knew what was going to grab you!"

I asked a clairvoyant for some insight into my terror as a child. Without knowing about my fears of the basement, she told me that she could see a dark room and an energetic being taking great delight in trying to frighten me as a young child. She described how it was trying to entangle me with something that looked like an orange Indian blanket. I immediately knew that she was speaking about the striped fabric partition separating the rooms in the basement. She saw the dirt crawlspace and explained that the energy had been trapped in our home when it was built. My brother and I were targeted because we were sensitive to energy and able to sense this being's presence. My teacher released the stuck energy from the home, which also helped heal the trauma that I had been carrying. Apparently, there was a reason that I panicked every time I went in our basement.

• • •

How do I know that what I experienced was real? What is the difference between a dream, a daydream, or an actual energetic or spiritual experience? Have I just been remembering a daydream all this time? Daydreams and dreams are easy to forget. I have found there is nothing to anchor them in my psyche, while real energetic phenomena and experiences with the paranormal are so profound that I remember them with explicit detail. I remember the feelings, the sights, sounds, and smells. And I remember my own visceral reaction. Recalling an intuitive energetic experience can bring me right back to the same fear, sadness, elation, or fight or flight response, including the quickened breathing and the elevated heart rate. It becomes hard to separate these experiences from my reality. So, they have become intertwined with my reality.

A note to parents: I wish my fears had been taken more seriously. If your child has a visceral fear reaction to something that you can't see, please do not automatically discount their experiences. Not everything can be seen by the naked eye; that doesn't mean it doesn't exist.

The Stanley Hotel

When I was a senior in high school, my mother thought it would be nice to spend the night away from home and share a bonding experience before I went off to college. We chose to spend the night at the Stanley Hotel in Estes Park, Colorado. Built in 1903, the Stanley Hotel was known for its paranormal activity, which wisely, my mother never told me ahead of time. I had no reason to be on alert energetically.

I had an uneasy feeling from the moment we walked through the front door. I attributed it to being a teenager in an old, dated hotel with my mother, where hopefully I wouldn't see anyone I knew. There were very few guests in the hotel, which was nice as far as going incognito, but as the evening wore on I would have preferred to have some more human company.

We started the evening with dinner in the almost empty dining room. The three-course dinner dragged on, which it would to any teen, and I wanted to be finished. But at the same time, I had no desire to go to our room. I cannot pinpoint any particular moment I became creeped out, but I sensed a very uncomfortable energetic disquiet throughout the hotel. I lingered around the hotel lobby looking at post cards, anything to stall the inevitable.

With no reason not to, we finally headed to our room for the night. As we wound our way down the creepy hallway, I felt the need to look back over my shoulder as we rounded each turn. Our floor was virtually deserted. I saw no one else on our floor the entire evening, so why they put us as far from the elevator as possible, and the perceived safety of others, was beyond me.

In the relative comfort of our room, my mother proceeded to fall asleep quickly. Dang! Not only was I already feeling anxious, but I was accustomed to the nocturnal hours of a teenager; my normal bedtime was typically not for a few more hours. Not able to keep the light on out of respect for my sleeping mother, I lay in the dark, unable to sleep. I heard noises and talking, yet it was obvious that they were not from floors above or below us, in the hallway, or in neighboring rooms. I felt the energetic presence of others in our room but in the dark, lit only by the light under the door from the hallway, saw no one. Needless to say, I barely slept at all that night while my mother slept beautifully.

I could not wait to leave in the morning and have not felt the need to return to The Stanley Hotel since. Later, when I asked my mother if she knew of the rumors that the hotel was haunted, she said yes. She chose to go there because she thought it would be fun to see if she noticed anything. Great.

A few years after our visit, The Stanley Hotel became the setting for Stephen King's *The Shining*. In retrospect, I am thankful I did not experience even more paranormal activity that night. Had I been truly frightened, I believe I would have completely shut the door to experiencing energy of any kind.

ANTIQUES AND ENERGY

I remember the first time that an antique shared its energy with me, or maybe it was just the first time that I actually noticed. I was in an antique furniture store and saw an attractive kitchen hutch made out of quarter-sawn oak. It was probably built between 1905 and 1910, stood about five feet tall, and had lots of shelves and beautiful original glass windows. While the piece was attractive, I found that I couldn't make myself go near it; I was having a visceral reaction to a piece of furniture! I was so stunned by my reaction to an inanimate object that I sat down at a nearby table to observe the hutch from a distance and try to understand what I was experiencing.

Suddenly, in my mind's eye, I saw the color hunter green and a man standing in a pool of blood in front of the hutch. The man looked to be in his mid-forties or -fifties, clean-cut, wearing a business suit and shoes from the 1950s or 60s. I sensed that the victim was female and had been shot. I had never seen a vision like that before and was a little freaked out, but also calmly intrigued. Certainly, if a gruesome scene like this had happened in front of the hutch, I supposed that the energy could be carried through the years in the wood and glass.

Just then another customer came over, looked at the hutch and said, "Whoa! What do you think happened near that piece? I don't know what it was, but it was something bad!" I was thankful that this gentleman had come by and validated that there was energy attached to the furniture and that I was sensing the energy correctly.

Now, before I buy something that was previously owned by someone else, I sense the energy to see if there's anything attached to it that I don't want in my home. Through my studies I have learned that I can clear this energy if I choose to.

KANSAS CITY

While in my thirties, I attended an educational conference in Kansas City, Missouri. Thankfully my husband Wayne accompanied me. Due to my last-minute registration, the hotels near the convention center were already booked. We ended up in a hotel a few miles away in a more industrial setting. The hotel's restaurant had a sign and an entrance from the street, but the hotel didn't have either a sign or its own door. This should have been my first clue that things might be amiss.

Clearly, the hotel had opened for convention traffic before it was ready for guests. The "lobby" was behind the restaurant, empty of other guests, and had a makeshift desk for checking in. When asked, the lone clerk explained that the hotel was recently renovated, but was not yet completed. We had to weave in and out of construction zones to get down a deserted corridor to find the elevator. On our floor, there was still more construction, no other guests, and our room was a great distance away from the elevator or any exit. Truly, had I been by myself, I never would have checked in.

Our hotel room had a large window, with drapes that did not adequately keep out the light from the city at night. It was possible to see the outline of everything in the room when the lights were off. I finally drifted off, despite being a light sleeper and feeling nervous that there were no other guests on our floor. The first night, I woke from a sound sleep when I felt someone sit on the bed next to my legs. The bed sagged under the weight of a heavy man. My eyes flew open knowing that my husband was lying next to me on the opposite side of the bed.

In the dim lighting, I saw the spirit form of a gentleman sitting on the bed right next to my knees. He was in his mid-fifties and was wearing black dress pants, a long-sleeved white dress shirt and a tie. He was tying his black dress shoes as if he was getting ready to go to a business meeting. His attire seemed to be from the 1960s. He stood up, walked toward the door and was gone. I woke Wayne who, of course, experienced nothing. Seeing this apparition made me quite anxious, but I relaxed when I realized that the gentleman did not seem to notice me or care that I was in the bed. In fact, I got the feeling that he had probably been a pretty nice guy, just a family man who had once stayed in this hotel on a business trip.

The same gentleman appeared before dawn the next morning, with the same clothes and the same calm demeanor. He dutifully sat down on the same spot on the bed to tie his shoes before he disappeared. This time I was not as frightened, but still apprehensive. Clearly this room was his, and in my mind, we were in his space.

On our last morning in the hotel, I went into the bathroom to take a shower. I closed the door behind me. The bathroom was excessively large and dimly lit. There was a claw foot bathtub in the middle of the room and a shower curtain hanging from the ceiling that fully engulfed the bathtub. There was room to walk completely around the bathtub on all sides.

As I showered in my dimly-lit shower curtain cocoon, I felt a rush of cool air as the shower curtain opened behind me. I felt the presence of someone standing there, watching me. The feeling was not that of a husband gazing lovingly at his wife, but rather of being stared at in a lascivious, lewd manner.

Cold from the continued draft, I quickly rinsed the shampoo out of my eyes. I cried to Wayne, "What are you doing?!" I turned around to speak to him, but there was no one there. Shaken to the core, I leapt out of the shower and sought my husband's company. He was in the bedroom and had not come into the bathroom at all. I did not have the same benevolent feeling from the shower visitor as I had from my 1960s businessman.

I was never so happy to leave a hotel in my life! As the bellman helped us with our luggage, I asked about my otherworldly visitors. He did not seem surprised. He explained that the building opened as a meat packing facility, and was transformed into a hotel in the 1960s. Over the years, it became rundown and eventually abandoned. Soon thereafter, the building was burned out and inhabited by transients and drug addicts. I was completely unnerved and so thankful to leave Kansas City.

Gettysburg

I spent many years in education, and my love for teaching spilled over into time with my daughters. One summer I thought we would explore American history, including slavery and the Civil War. We drove to Gettysburg, Pennsylvania. It was inspiring being on one of the battlefields where part of the Civil War had taken place. Rather unassuming, it looked like any other field before the hay had been cut. The feeling it invoked, however, was a very strong sense of suffering and death. In my mind's eye I saw the battlefield with wounded and dying soldiers strewn about. Maybe I had seen too many Civil War movies, because my brain filled in all the blanks.

Throughout Gettysburg, I clearly felt like there were souls everywhere and some of them wanted to be noticed and acknowledged. Walking downtown around Lincoln Square, I was surprised that we were almost the only ones on the street. I expected Gettysburg to be more of a popular tourist attraction than it was. As we approached the statue of Abraham Lincoln, someone bumped into me. I turned around to see who it was and there was no one there. I clearly felt someone in my space; the person was so close to me energetically that I felt like I needed to take a step back to get out of his space. I sensed an old-timey male presence that was a few inches taller than I, wearing a dirty brown thigh-length coat and dirty, worn leather boots. I felt that he was very annoyed with my presence.

As we continued to walk, I felt the intense, direct gaze of someone watching us from a second-floor window nearby. I stood still, trying to detect any movement in the window. After a few minutes, I realized there was no one on the second floor looking down. Interestingly, I later read about President Lincoln preparing the Gettysburg Address from a second story bedroom at the David Wills House, close to where we had been standing.

WITNESS TO A CRIME?

One day, we were shopping in Denver for antiques and we entered a store that was new to us. I am not sure what the building was originally built for, but it was obvious that it had seen better days, as had its industrial neighborhood. The building had been refurbished in the hopes of starting to bring fresh life to the community.

We walked in the door and I was immediately struck with an uneasy feeling. I was on energetic high alert, but I wasn't sure why. In the middle of the room was a large white marble staircase that cascaded down to the first floor. From the top of the stairs, one could see much of the first floor below.

I had a vision that I tried to ignore, but it insisted on being seen. I saw this same building in earlier, derelict times: broken windows, graffiti-covered walls, filth and rubbish on the floor. There was no electricity. Drug addicts took refuge inside the dark basement, knowing that no one would come looking for them there. At the bottom of the stairs I saw a mattress. It was old, stained, and strewn with drug paraphernalia. I saw what I guessed to be the remnants of heroin or meth use. I saw a young woman in her twenties lying on the mattress; she was partially nude, unconscious or dead. Her stringy, dirty-blonde hair lay flat against her white skin. Her wrists had been tied to the stair rail and it was apparent that she had suffered greatly at the hands of someone else. The emotional grief, despair, and panic of being held captive and eventually abandoned were energetically pulsing throughout the building and in my head.

I could not make myself stay in the store and we left immediately. This scene was so real in my head that I contemplated calling the police to report the crime. But what would I even say? I had no evidence that such a crime had taken place, nor a year I thought it might have happened. I had no information about the guilty party, just a vision of the victim. I was not a psychic or medium, just someone who "saw" something I wished I hadn't.

I had no idea what to do with the information I had gleaned from being in the store. So, I did nothing, other than be more sure of my ability to sense energy that was left behind from earlier times.

Italian Mafia

The west coast has always been a favorite destination of mine. Once, while on vacation in San Francisco, we were eating at Alioto's, an iconic Italian restaurant at Fisherman's Wharf. I excused myself to use the restroom and went upstairs. On my way back down the dimly lit stairwell, I stopped short in my tracks.

In front of me, at the bottom of the stairs, was a horrific, grisly murder scene. I saw a Caucasian man in a business suit curled up in a pool of blood having been shot multiple times. I saw the picture clear as day. I was given the impression that it was a mob or mafia style "hit" that took place sometime in the 1950s or 60s. I saw the vision in black-and-white as if it was an old newspaper photograph. I was careful as I continued walking down the stairs to steer clear of the area where the murder had taken place. The vision was so realistic that I did not want to get blood on my shoes. I was not frightened by the vision but intrigued by what I was seeing and why I was seeing it.

Years later I read the history of Alioto's Restaurant. Dating back to 1925, Nunzio Alioto opened a fresh fish stall, which grew into Alioto's Restaurant in the 1930s. His brother, Giuseppe Alioto, founded the famous Fisherman's Wharf in the 1930s along with his partner Francesco Lanza, the first real crime boss of San Francisco. I did not see evidence online of any murders taking place inside Alioto's, although the family's ties to the mob were well known.

The Olde House

One spring, our family travelled to North Carolina with my sister to visit her in-laws, Drew, Buddy and Dicie. They had a century-old home, lovingly called "The Olde House," with a backyard bordering on the Shallotte River. During the day, we enjoyed the sprawling grounds and the splintered dock on the river. However, in the evening, my enthusiasm waned. Our little family slept upstairs while my sister and her in-laws slept on the main floor. To be more exact, my husband and daughters slept upstairs while I sat vigilantly awake, unable to sleep because of the apparitions moving throughout the home. The bedroom next door to us had a foreboding energy to it and I stayed away as much as I could. The one time I did walk by, I happened to glance inside. I saw the spirit of an elderly woman sitting at a vanity table, combing her hair in the mirror. I quickly moved on and went downstairs.

In our bedroom, there was a great deal of moving energy. I never felt like we were the only ones upstairs, although in the physical sense, we were. One evening, I saw what seemed to be the spirit of a Confederate soldier, dressed in gray, gazing out of our bedroom window toward the river. A woman was standing behind him, wearing a yellow dress of the same time period. She was hugging the soldier from behind, also looking out the window.

When I asked Dicie and Drew if they had ever noticed anything strange in The Olde House, they said no. Several of their friends, however, claimed that the home was haunted after hearing footsteps and smelling a strange odor near the stairs. Drew added that workmen told her of seeing apparitions, and hearing male and female voices when no one else was in the house.

THE ALAMO

A work conference called me to San Antonio, Texas and the site where the Battle of the Alamo took place. During my entire trip, I was aware of being surrounded by the energy of soldiers that had lived and died, but were still lingering nearby. I visited the tourist sites; although there were not many tourists, I felt like I was walking through an extremely crowded venue. The spirit life around me was so thick and rich I almost felt claustrophobic.

With some spare time on my hands, I entered a large chain bookstore at the nearby mall. I walked into a section of the store that was ice cold. I commented to the store clerk about the excessive air conditioning. He responded that was not the air conditioning, but the store was located on one of the Alamo battlefields and intuitive customers reported feeling cold energy from the deceased soldiers. I thought if he could be nonchalant about it, I could as well.

The hotel was similarly full of energy. I could hardly sleep in my room because of a strong swirling sensation of unseen energy that continued throughout the night. It always felt like there were other people with me even when I was alone in my room. The busiest times appeared to be between two and four in the morning. I remember waking up and thinking that the hotel cleaning staff was in the room vacuuming and talking. Of course they weren't; it was the middle of the night. But the room had visitors, nonetheless.

ELIZABETH AND THE CROW

One day, I was driving across town for work. Out of nowhere I started feeling melancholy, gloomy, and almost despondent. I started to weep. I had no idea what had come over me. Not accustomed to energy work, I wondered what was happening. I saw a vision of a funeral and a coffin with a man inside it. I thought, OK, someone died. But, I didn't normally see things or have visions, so what was going on?

At my destination, I composed myself and exited my car. In a high branch of a nearby tree there was an extremely loud crow. In fact, it was so loud, it seemed like it really wanted my attention. How could an ordinary crow be that loud? I had never energetically spoken to an animal before. Hoping to not be seen by colleagues, I found myself saying out loud, "Seriously, what do you want?!" I received a message that the man I saw in the coffin had passed away much too soon, leaving behind a young family, totally in shock and unprepared. I had no idea what to do with this information. I completed my business and headed back to my office. It was difficult for me to shake the emotions and visions that I had just seen and heard.

When I returned to my office I discovered that my co-worker Elizabeth had been notified that morning that her husband Charlie had died of a heart attack while at work. Charlie was in his mid-forties and left behind two young sons and a devastated wife.

It took me almost ten years before I was comfortable telling Elizabeth the story of the crow's message. By that time, her boys had grown up and she had found love with a wonderful new husband. Why did I wait so long to tell her? I waited because I had no understanding or explanation for why or how the message had been shared with me. Why did I finally choose to tell her? Because I had just been establishing my spiritual legs and wanted to share that part of my journey with her in case, somehow, it could bring her comfort and bring me closure.

A Life in Review

My mother-in-law, Helen, passed away at age seventy-eight after a long struggle with cancer. Her funeral was held in her small hometown funeral home. As I sat in the front row, my attention kept getting pulled to the front left corner of the pulpit. I literally could not keep my focus on the speaker or the soloist, as there was an energetic presence that I could not stop watching. I saw Helen in spirit and some sort of etheric guide standing together, looking out toward the congregation. I understood that the guide was helping Helen take stock of this life that she had lived. They showed no emotion or judgment. I thought it intriguing that those of us seated in the congregation were still wrought with raw grief at her passing and our loss and here she was observing, detached from any emotion. The guide motioned with his arm to draw Helen's attention to the crowd. I understood that it was showing Helen the people who gathered in her honor, and it was discussing the impact she had made on us all. I felt her presence so strongly in that corner of the room that I blew her a kiss.

Cocooning

I had an incredibly vivid dream about three weeks after my mother-in-law passed away. I dreamt that I went to an apartment and a middle-aged gentleman who was in an army uniform from the early 1900s answered the door. He took me to a back room where Mom was sleeping on the couch. She woke and spoke, but not to anyone in particular. She said she had been exhausted and was sleeping most of the time. The word that came to my mind was "cocooning." She was cocooning and resting after her very difficult struggle with cancer and her passing. I was not sure who the gentleman was, if he had been a relative in the past or was some sort of guide. I got the feeling that he was keeping watch over her while she healed and gathered strength. I also sensed that he and Helen had known each other before.

I was clear that Helen was safe, transitioning, and letting me know that she was OK.

When I woke, I burst into tears. My dream was so real. I knew I had received an amazing gift. I got to see Mom again, a woman I cherished for the last twelve years and had lost. I was also given insight that there was life for a soul after life as we know it.

. . .

These experiences left me wondering. Why am I seeing and feeling these things while no one around me sees the same things? Do these visions mean I am psychic? The negative cultural perception connected to the word "psychic" had me spinning. What do I do with this? What do I want to do with this? If I want to explore it, what do I do and who do I do it with?

Growing up Methodist, I had heard skepticism about psychic or intuitive abilities. Isn't there something in the Bible that says this level of knowledge is wrong? Or worse, evil? For something to be wrong, doesn't there need to be an intention of wrongdoing? I never intended to be able to access psychic phenomena; it was just there.

Did having this ability, whether it was wanted or not, distance me from God? The God I love and have a personal relationship with? I think the Bible would make us think so. I still went to church. And sometimes at church I saw spirit forms that I did not intend or desire to see. How ironic. If seeing energy is wrong, why was it happening at church?

Clearly, I had more questions than answers.

I did not speak very often of the visions I saw, things I felt or heard. My friends did not understand and found it a little spooky. I realized that unless someone had received information intuitively themselves, they could not understand what I had experienced. When I did run across someone who shared similar experiences, it felt like a salve on an open wound to be able to ask questions and share stories.

I have been fortunate to not be deluged with many visions of murders or horrific scenes as some intuitives describe. I have seen just enough in my lifetime to leave me intrigued, and wanting to learn more.

CHAPTER 2

Sylvia

How lucky I was to get to know and love Sylvia! We taught together in an elementary school in Los Angeles and became family quickly in spite of, or maybe because of, our twenty-three-year age difference. I was in my late twenties and Sylvia her young fifties. While recovering from my divorce, Sylvia became my best friend, my mother, my sister, my cheerleader, and my travel partner. Sylvia's husband Cliff became my dear, dear friend and partner in crime. I became the daughter that they never had.

Feeling the need to re-create my life in 1990, I moved to Colorado to be closer to my family, but my relationship with Sylvia was stronger than ever. She and Cliff drove across the country to help me renovate my new home. We had a great month filled with laughter and very little sleep. Several times a year, we traveled together or spent extended time together at each other's homes. My mantra was "Friends are Chosen Family" and somehow, Sylvia and Cliff felt closer than the family I was born into.

Over the years, our relationship deepened. Sylvia and Cliff joined us for holidays and important family functions, including my second wedding. My youngest daughter was named after Sylvia. As a new mother, I shared all of my daughters' developmental milestones and photos with Sylvia, and when I needed parenting advice or a loving hello, she was the first person I called.

Thanksgivings, Sylvia flew my direction and we cooked Thanksgiving dinner together for approximately twenty-five friends and family members. I was the cook and she was my sous chef. We enjoyed this tradition together for many years, and it became one of my favorite times of the year. I always felt completely surrounded by the love and companionship of my dear friend. As Sylvia got older, her role at Thanksgiving became more that of chief dishwasher and late night cheerleader as I resumed the preparation and cooking. But it was all good!

December 2009, Cliff died unexpectedly from a heart attack. Having been married for forty-five years, Sylvia was thrust into widowhood, which she was not prepared for and did not want to embrace. Our roles quickly shifted and I became her teacher (how to cook and use the internet) and her escape when she just couldn't stand to be in her home alone anymore. Sylvia and I spent more time together as we both tried to fill the void of Cliff's passing.

The Premonition

In November of 2013, Sylvia's brother was dying of cancer and she knew she needed to stay closer to home for Thanksgiving in case she needed to go be with him. Of course, I was crushed but I completely understood. That Thanksgiving morning, I woke having had the worst dream ever. In my dream, her sister-in-law Charlotte called me and told me that Sylvia was in the hospital with an incurable illness and was dying. I couldn't shake the dread and sadness of that dream throughout our Thanksgiving Day. I tried to call Sylvia a couple of times, but I knew that she would be spending the holiday at a relative's house and I wouldn't be able to reach her.

The next morning, my dream became my real-life nightmare. I received a call from Sylvia's sister-in-law and was told that my dear friend had had a stroke at the Thanksgiving dinner table. She was in a hospital in Los Angeles. I immediately flew to be by her side and realized that the stroke was more massive than previously thought. My beautiful, vibrant, seventy-five-year-old friend was completely incapacitated. Heartbroken, I called her brother to let him know that, as her Power of Attorney, it was time for him to step up to take control. Within a few days, Sylvia was transferred to a nursing home with complete paralysis of the left side of her body.

In my devastation and hopelessness, I was also stunned by the fact that I had received the news of Sylvia's Illness before the stroke happened. I knew that I was truly connected to her, but I did not know this kind of communication was even a possibility.

No Road to Recovery

As she tried to recover from the stroke, we were all saddened and frustrated that Sylvia wasn't getting better. There was very little improvement, if any. But she never gave up hope. Ever.

Over the course of the next few months I would return to my family and work and then fly out to spend time with Sylvia. One day in the nursing home, the nurse asked if Sylvia had any children. My response was, "Just me!" Sylvia smiled and nodded her head. I stopped at Sylvia's house to pick up a few items for her. I looked around and saw photos all over her bookcases and desktop including several of her nieces and nephews and family members that had passed away. I was particularly touched to see that at least half of her photos were of me and my family or of our travels together. I was clear that I had always thought the world of Sylvia. It was very special to see that the depth of my feelings was returned.

Back in Colorado, I kept getting intuitive information about Sylvia's health before the doctors would find the issue. I heard that Sylvia was going to get pneumonia. I called her sister-in-law and asked for someone to please check Sylvia's lungs. Two days later I was informed that Sylvia had been diagnosed with pneumonia.

Then Sylvia started having issues with her stomach. She had contracted C. *difficile* (a bacterial infection) in the nursing home. Sylvia was placed in the hospital as the nursing home could no longer treat her. C. *difficile* is extremely contagious and anyone visiting her had to gown up. I visited Sylvia every few weeks in the hospital. Her health continued to decline.

The Prognosis

After three months of paralysis and illness, I was with Sylvia when her doctor came in and told her that she had been diagnosed with stomach cancer and would not be getting any better. In fact, there were no treatments that she could survive that would add more time to her life. The only thing left was to try to help manage her pain. The doctor told me that death was imminent. She did not tell Sylvia, nor did Sylvia ask.

Three long weeks later, Sylvia was still fighting to survive and had not given up on the hope of a miracle. Her friends and family members had all been to see her. They had already all accepted that there would be no miracles coming.

March 13, 2013. The days leading up to Sylvia's passing were excruciating to witness; I cannot even fathom what her personal experience was like. While nurses tried their best to keep her physical discomfort to a minimum, clearly she was uncomfortable and in pain. Sylvia kept fighting to live even when the doctors told me they thought she would have passed away already and they had never seen anyone fight so hard to stay alive before.

March 14, 2013. I was sitting by Sylvia's hospital bed while she floated in and out of consciousness. My eyes were transfixed down the hallway, yet focusing on nothing. My attention was caught by an older Asian gentleman walking down the hallway toward her room. I burst into tears as I recognized Sylvia's husband Cliff, who had passed away three years before in the same hospital. There he was in his favorite jeans and Hawaiian print shirt, looking larger than life. I did not want to take my eyes off him because I knew he would go as easily as he came. When I finally blinked, Cliff was no longer visible. My tears were partly because I missed Cliff terribly, but also because his visit was a sure sign that Sylvia's time was limited.

Later that evening as I sat with Sylvia and rubbed lotion onto her hands and arms, I sensed the spirit forms of her mother and father outside of her hospital room, looking in. Selfishly, I said, "You can't have her yet. She is with me now." I was jealously guarding every minute that her spirit was still with me.

March 15, 2013. Early that morning, I walked into Sylvia's room while she slept. Not wanting to wake her, I busied myself straightening up her room, watering plants and removing dead flowers. I watched as she slept. Suddenly, she started choking from the fluid building up in her lungs. Sylvia was silently panicking. As I raised the head of her bed, I said "Syl, it's Ruth. I'm right here with you. I'm calling for the nurse." I felt her relax knowing I was beside her. It was good to know that even though she was no longer speaking, she was able to hear and understand what was being said to her.

At that moment, Sylvia's energy shifted from wanting to live, to wanting to die. The rest of the day it felt as if her spirit would come and go from her struggling body. I felt that my role shifted as well, from protector and guardian keeping her body safe, to that of coach, encouraging her and keeping her surroundings quiet and loving while her soul passed from her body. Later that evening, her niece Kimberly and I by her side, Sylvia took her last breath. She was finally free to be with Cliff and her family members on the other side.

Alone But Not Lonely

March 16, 2013. I woke up the next morning, having barely slept and feeling hung over, with the day before playing through my mind over and over. I packed my bag and started driving to the airport so I could return to my family. Driving on the Los Angeles freeway, I started crying, sobbing uncontrollably. I started talking out loud, even though no one was there to hear it. I told Sylvia all of my thoughts, regrets of her terrible last few months, and abject terror of living life without her. I sobbed out my disappointment that she would not see my girls grow up and that she would not be moving closer to me so I could enjoy spending time with her during my retirement, as we had planned. I yelled my apologies that I had been unable to save her, unable to provide the miracle that she had been counting on. I struggled to see the road through tears that flowed and hoped that drivers in the next lane were not watching my complete breakdown. My cathartic outbursts continued. If only Sylvia could hear me!

I felt a presence in the back seat, as if someone were riding with me. In shock, I stopped talking. I might have stopped breathing as well. If there was someone in the back seat, what should I do? My mind raced. Should I pull off the busy freeway? Keep driving to a police station? I didn't know my way around Los Angeles, and I could tell this wasn't going to end well. was terrified. I looked in the rear-view mirror afraid of what or who I might see.

Instead of a dangerous stranger, I saw the most beautiful gift anyone could have ever given me. In the back seat, sitting close together were Sylvia and Cliff in spirit. They looked younger than when they died. Sylvie looked a little dazed and tired, but Cliff looked so content. I laughed through my tears. I knew it was preposterous that I was receiving this visitation, but I didn't care. I soaked up every minute of it. I thought of the movie *Driving Miss Daisy*, and laughed at the oddity of my chauffeuring the spirits of my two dearest friends around Los Angeles.

Seeing Sylvia and Cliff together, both having transcended through the trauma of illness and death, helped to heal the raw pain I had been carrying. They were both fine and going to be together in a good place. They showed me that they would always be there with me, whenever I needed them. I felt such love and healing. I would not have to wait to be reunited with them, as they were never leaving me. Awesome!

After the Passing

When I returned to Colorado, I felt Sylvia all through my house, particularly in the living room and in "her" bedroom, otherwise known as our guest room. My suspicions were confirmed when I watched our white cockapoo, Jack. A true lap dog, Jack was typically in our laps or at our feet; he was always in the same room with us. After Sylvia's passing, there were times that I would hear Jack making noises in the living room. He would be sitting in the living room by himself, on the third stair. When I called him, he was frozen, not in a scared way, but in an "I'm not budging" way. He was not barking or growling, but whining excitedly. I could then see Sylvia in spirit, sitting with Jack, petting him, and talking with him. I told Sylvia that she was welcome to stay in my home as long as she needed to. She was always welcome.

A Celebration of Life

I had the tremendous honor of organizing Sylvia's Celebration of Life that was held in Los Angeles. I spoke out loud to her as I chose songs, picked eulogy speakers, decided on flowers, and crafted the written program. I received so much feedback energetically from her during this process that it felt like Sylvia was sitting right next to me, planning her own funeral.

Was it just that I knew her so well that I was able to anticipate her comments? No, I actually received her answers! I would hear myself saying things like, "Syl, what do you think of the Old Rugged Cross? Or how about Amazing Grace?" I felt a quiet dis-ease when she did not like my choice, and a confident rush of energy when I got it right. In my head, not my ears, I heard, "That's a good one!" and "I played that for Cliff's funeral." It wasn't enough to have picked the right song title, then we had to pick the right recording artist and version. I played many different recordings of each of the songs she wanted, until I finally had Sylvia's go-ahead on each recorded song.

While wading through photos for the slide show, Sylvia had a lot of opinions. I heard, "Keep looking," "What about the ones you took at Lake Tahoe?" and "Isn't there one where I'm not wearing sun glasses?" My favorite was, "Gee, thanks a lot!" which was one of Sylvia's trademark sayings, when I liked a photo that she thought was not very flattering.

Putting together the written program was a fascinating experience! Sylvia and I had created several photo books together, so I was used to her sitting down beside me, looking over my shoulder, and helping me select the font, font size, colors, and photos. Sylvia had an amazing knack for sticking with a project until it met with her approval and looked flawless. Creating the slideshow and the written program for her funeral was no different. When I tried out different fonts, I heard things like, "That's too curly" or "That's too blocky." We finally settled on just the right font. Then I had to make the font larger, then smaller until we settled on just the right size.

Choosing the color of the ink could have been easier, as I would have gone with basic black. But Sylvia had other ideas. I tried to save the program file using black letters and my computer literally would not save it. I changed the letters to midnight blue and amazingly I could save the file. So, I stuck with midnight blue, which was one of Sylvia's favorite colors.

Having Sylvia help me plan her funeral was an incredibly beautiful gift. I laughed and shed a great many bittersweet tears during the process. When it was all said and done, Sylvia's hand was evident throughout her Celebration of Life. Her friends and sisters came up to me afterwards and said the service was amazing, that it felt like Sylvia was in the room right along with us. And I believe that she was.

A few months later, I carried Sylvia's ashes to Honolulu for a smaller family funeral, where her ashes would be interred. After caring for Sylvia through good and terrible health, her passing, and even for her ashes at the end, I was completely heartbroken that this era of my life had come to an end. At the Honolulu airport, waiting to fly home after the service, I felt such tremendous loss at leaving my dear friend's ashes that I could not fully inhale or exhale for fear of sobbing out loud. My husband Wayne handed me a package that my sister had sent along to give me at that very moment. I opened a padded envelope and found a necklace of strung glass beads. Each bead contained a small amount of Sylvia's ashes, which my sister had taken without my knowledge and given to a glass blower. The beads were purple, black, and blue and had gray ash swirls throughout. At that point I wept, much to my daughters' consternation. Words cannot express the gratitude, immense sadness, yet contentment that I felt at that moment. I did not have to leave Sylvia in Honolulu; I was taking part of her home with me.

Next Steps

I have never had a relationship where I felt such a strong connection. Losing Sylvia physically was devastating. Since her passing three years ago, I have found that my connection to my dear friend still exists. She has come to me many times and I was told just recently that Sylvia is connected to my heart chakra with a golden cord. My heart has always known this, and it brings me joy, tears to my eyes, and appreciation for a love I never thought I could know.

I don't know if Sylvia's spirit has some mystical ability that other spirits don't have. Maybe all of our loved ones who have passed on have the ability to be right next to us in spirit when we call. Or is it that I was open and happened to have the ability to see and feel her when she presented herself? Either way, I love it and would not change a thing.

My ability to connect with Sylvia while she was in body across the nation, and later with her spirit after her passing, really made me want to learn more about this spiritual connection and my role in it. I have since devoted my time and energy to take intuitive and clairvoyant classes and wallow in all things related to spiritual energy. As a result, I have experienced a personal transformation that surprises me and those who know me well. I have learned a lot about my soul's purpose for this lifetime. I have learned that my life to date has been leading up to a future of teaching, healing, and soul to soul connection. I don't think I would have gotten to this point without the soul to soul communication I shared with Sylvia.

CHAPTER
3

Learning to See with New Eyes

Sylvia's passing prompted a few visits with intuitive readers and healers. I was desperate to understand my intuitive connection to her, as well as my earlier experiences. Over the course of two years, I sought out four different professionals: Leanne Holitza from Insightful Inspirations, Shawna Reininger of The Conscious Enterprise, Lauren Skye with Inner Connection Institute, and Stacia Synnestvedt, The Meditating Mama. They each had spiritual gifts that defied reason. They answered questions and I experienced healing at a deep level within a few hours. I know that level of healing could not have been possible through years of traditional talk therapy. I am eternally grateful to these ladies for their support and guidance!

Wanting to understand more, I gravitated to books on psychic phenomena and metaphysical concepts. I read books by Sylvia Browne, John Edward and Theresa Caputo. Personalities and reputations notwithstanding, I could resonate with their abilities to communicate with Spirit. I also picked up a class here and there on basic energy reading. Much of what I had experienced in the past was beginning to make sense to me.

Past Lives

Past lives? Is it possible that Sylvia and I had a past life together, or several? I had heard a little about past lives before, but I just thought it had to do with reincarnation and was not something I believed in or was intrigued by. But somehow, after listening to Leanne Holitza talking about Sylvia, Cliff, and I being together in a past life, the idea started to resonate with me. I never understood the closeness that we shared; it made no sense for as short a time as I had known them. I was completely at ease with them and instinctively knew I could trust them with my life.

Thinking about whether or not I believed I had had past lives, I was reminded of the time I met a gentleman named Randy. He taught a leadership seminar that I attended in California. The minute I saw him, I knew that this was not my first encounter with him. How could I have known him? I had a five-hour commute to get to the conference; there was no possible way I had met him before. But in my heart of hearts I knew him on a deeper soul level. I could literally see that I had been his wife and we had lived in a log cabin as farmers in a much less complicated time. Neighbors were few and far between and we relied on each other for companionship and comfort. I could see his red flannel shirt and his mustache. After the conference, I struck up a conversation and we became fast friends. His personality, morals, and values were exactly that of the man I "remembered." Here I was twenty-three years later sitting with Leanne, hearing about Sylvic and a past life, so I asked about Randy. Without my going into details, she described the same past life scenario that I had pictured on my own.

I have had several intuitives tell me that I had a past life as a medicine woman or intuitive healer. I was killed for my choice of vocation, which would explain my reticence to go head first into my own psychic abilities during this lifetime. They also all mentioned a past life as a nun, which is no surprise, as I have had a very strong pull to the Divine much of my life.

I now believe in past lives. I don't know where that fits in with Methodist theology; it probably doesn't. But it works for me. So, I have adopted it as part of my own theology. I have learned that unfounded fears such as swimming in the ocean, déjà vu when meeting a stranger, or that inexplicable desire or "need" to travel to a particular location over and over may indicate that a past life is influencing a person.

Good to See You Again, or Maybe Not

Sometimes seeing someone from a past life is not a pleasant experience. Like a bad penny, they just won't go away. My friend Marie married her "bad penny," not once, but twice, in this lifetime alone! She said she hated him the first time they got divorced, so what in the world possessed her to marry him a second time? Knowing he was not dangerous and wanting to support her, we all smiled and looked the other way.

Then we saw the second divorce. This time it was less amicable. Marie not only said she really hated Steven this time, but was now also afraid of him. Apparently not everyone gets better with age.

Did they have a soul contract that kept them coming into each other's lives, even when it was not healthy? At Marie's request, I used a new skill and did a past life reading on her and Steven. I saw that they had indeed been in a few past lives together. In each lifetime they were together, then apart, then back together again. No matter how ugly or egregious their behaviors were to each other, it was as if all had been forgotten and they had permission to return at any time. Soul to soul, that was their pattern. Had we known this, the rest of us would not have been surprised when he showed back up on her doorstep.

I also knew Marie's bad penny. I only saw Steven a few times a year, but I saw him year after year. I was never particularly comfortable or uncomfortable around him, but he was not easy to talk with and was quite opinionated. I could tell Marie was happy when she divorced him for the second time, so I supported her decision.

Hearing that things were not going well for Steven with the second divorce, I was surprised and a little uneasy when he showed up at *my* house. Luckily we were not home. I had an vulnerable and agitated feeling and tried to energetically read his motive for dropping by. I was unable to; all I could see was swirling, really angry energy.

I had a past life reading done to see if there was a reason I was anxious and unable to read Steven's energy. My teacher Stacia saw that I shared a past life with him as well. In another lifetime, he strangled me, maybe not to the point of death, but certainly to the point of extreme fear. My cellular memory in this body recalled the fear, which left me feeling vulnerable and unable to get a clear reading on his energy or motive. Thankfully, she saw that his purpose for the house call was one of seeking answers and not one of hostility.

All In the Family

I have read that in spirit, we tend to hang around the same group of souls lifetime after lifetime. This ideology makes sense for me and Sylvia, and also for Marie and Steven. For the most part, I welcome that idea. It brings me comfort knowing that I will be seeing my loved ones again and again.

I have also read that before we enter (and subsequently re-enter) this world in physical form, our souls convene on the "Threshold," the space where souls linger before birth, after death, and between lifetimes. Each of us, in spirit form, determines what we need to learn in this upcoming lifetime and how we will go about learning it. The theory also states that together, a group of souls decide what roles they will play in each others' lives—sometimes loving and benevolent, and other times not. In other words, we choose our parents, friends, and foes before we are ever born.

The conversation with our soul companions might go like this:

Soul 1: "OK, this time, I need to learn forgiveness. I want to be a woman and an artist. I don't want to worry about finances this time. I need to have parents and a husband that keep me comfortable."

Soul 2: "Great! I will be your first love and then we'll get married. As your husband, I will have a job that pays really well. Let's have two amazing kids and then when you turn fifty and are feeling most vulnerable, I will have an affair and make child custody issues really ugly. You can work on forgiving me."

Soul 1: "Ugh, thanks! What are you going to work on?"

Soul 2: "Humility."

Soul 3: "I can help with that! I can be the woman you have the affair with, and then after you leave your wife I can dump you for a younger, richer man, leaving you with nobody."

Soul 4: "And I can be your boss and keep emasculating you at every turn. When your mistress dumps you, I can fire you, accusing you of misappropriating funds. Of course, you didn't do it, but that will make it difficult for you to get a good paying job, plunging you into financial despair. That should help you with humility."

Soul 2: "Ouch! Thanks! What are you going to be working on?"

Soul 3: "I need to learn self-reliance, so maybe I should have emotionally distant parents and a string of bound-to-fail relationships. Maybe I should throw in some health concerns, nothing major, but just enough to help me feel vulnerable with no one to count on. I will *have* to learn to rely on myself."

Soul 5: "Got you covered! I can be your dad, and your twin sister who murdered you in your last lifetime can be your mom this time around. That might feel a little confusing at times, but you two still have unfinished business to work on. I am going to be a minister because I need to work on my relationship with God. I will be extremely judgmental and too busy with my congregation to spend much time with you, so we have the distant parent thing taken care of!"

So, really? People who are mean and do awful things to us are in our lives for a reason? Maybe so. In those cases, I suppose I should learn to be grateful for their presence in my life, as apparently, they are providing a life lesson that I need to learn.

Where does this theology put us with horrific situations like rape, murder, or the Holocaust? I have no clue. Did all of those souls think the death marches, starvation, and dying at the hands of Nazi soldiers was a good idea? I doubt it. Does one person's mental illness get to outweigh all of the life lessons and opportunities that others had created on the Threshold before life began? Someday I hope to know the answer.

HEALING MASTERS

One of the first courses I took was with Shawna Reininger. This course was on basic energy awareness. An element of the course was receiving a Healing Master, a being that works specifically with one person and can provide healing for chakras and emotions on an energetic level. I had heard about healing guides before and was anxiously waiting to experience one.

Going into the class I was quite intimidated because I imagined other students had more experience and a foundation for reading energy. During guided meditation, Shawna instructed us to put a piece of paper on the floor in front of us and to call in our healing master. I had no idea what to expect, but imagined I would see a figure at least as tall as me. My bigger fear was that I would see nothing. With my eyes closed, I sensed a presence in front of me, but it was not in human form. I saw a tornado about a foot tall that was the color of Spanish moss. I was not sure if this was a healing master or not.

I told Shawna I wasn't seeing anything and she said, "Are you sure?" No, I wasn't sure. I was seeing something, just not what I was hoping for. I decided this must be my healing master after all. I asked it what it wanted to be called. I heard the word "Peas." I thought that was humorous because the moss green color certainly did look like mashed peas.

I started working with Peas, mostly sending healing to myself. Self-serving, yes, but that was all I knew how to do. As I became more confident, I asked Peas to assist in tragedies in the news and among friends, as much as they could accept his help.

ENERGETIC HOME CLEARING

When my daughter was younger, she refused to sleep in her room. As a matter of fact, she refused to be upstairs by herself or even go into her bedroom by herself. One day she ran down the stairs screaming at the top of her lungs. I asked her why she was making so much noise. She explained, "The ghosts don't like it when I make a lot of noise!" I told a friend and she suggested I have someone come provide a house clearing. Intrigued, I signed up. Judith Magnum came to the house, read the energy, and explained that at one time a farmer and his four family members had perished on our property in a house fire. Judith took me into my daughter's bedroom and said that she experienced this family's energy right at the head of my daughter's bed. Apparently, my daughter was very sensitive to these external energies.

Drinks Anyone?

Shortly thereafter, we purchased a different home and I was very excited about spending some time renovating it prior to moving in. The more time we spent inside the house, the more I thought about throwing parties for friends and about including alcohol on the menu. I bought several kinds of beer, wine, and mixed drinks in preparation for having friends over. This was odd, because I'm not much of a drinker, and neither is my husband. I almost never drink at home and typically don't serve much alcohol when company comes over.

We went on vacation, and while in Florida I requested that we visit a local winery. I proceeded to buy a case of sweet wines and matching flavored fruit smoothie mixes for friends to enjoy in our new home. I could envision friends sitting on our back deck enjoying their drinks, while I blended up fresh batches of the wine smoothie drinks. I could see myself having one too many of the frozen drinks, because they would be icy cold and sweet, not really like drinking alcohol at all.

Even though we would not be moving into our new home for another nine months, I had the wines shipped to our transitional rental home. I knew that we would not open a single bottle while living in our rental home, as it just didn't seem to be *that* kind of a house. While I physically went along with the shopping and the purchases, I was actually very confused by my strong desire to surround myself in all this alcohol. Our friends and relatives are not wine drinkers or fruit/alcohol smoothie drinkers.

My own behaviors related to drinking alcohol in the new house were not making any sense to me! I asked Lauren Skye for an energy reading of our new home. She could see that the previous family had a teenager who had a problem with alcohol addiction. She would hide alcohol throughout the house and then sneak around to drink it without getting caught. I had the energy cleared from the home and my desire to stockpile alcohol completely disappeared! The fruit smoothie mixes rotted without ever being opened and I ended up throwing them all away. Friends and family came over and, while we offered a few beers or wine, the majority of folks drank sodas or sparkling flavored waters. I experienced firsthand my desires and behaviors being altered by existing energy in our home. I can only imagine what toll that addictive energy could have had on our teenage daughters living in this home day after day.

If These Walls Could Talk

The home we renovated was over twenty years old; two families had lived in it prior to our taking ownership. Through the yearlong construction, we took several walls down to the studs and replaced all of the windows. Wayne and I checked on the project frequently and got to know each of the subcontractors.

Each night we came into the house to see what progress had been made. Perhaps most interesting to me was that I could walk in and sense which workers had been in the home based on the residual energy they left behind. If the energy was enthusiastic and positive, I knew that Casey and Mark had been there. Al left plodding and methodical energy. If it was heavy and depressive, then Glenn had been on site. Chris, our General Contractor, left the home feeling as if contemplative and thorough thinking had taken place. Having learned how to clear energy from homes in my coursework, I made it a habit to clear the energy of the workmen every time I came into the house. I always followed up with filling and surrounding the home with the desired energies of skilled craftsmanship, expediency, a sense of family, and lastly, health and safety.

About halfway through the project, I walked into the home and started to cry. Not because of the mess surrounding me, but because of the feeling of utter despair that was emanating from the house. Even Wayne, who is not all that attuned to energy, said, "It feels like the house is crying." I immediately sat down and listened to the energy. I heard that the home had provided a place of love and security for the two previous families. Now that we had taken it down to the studs, it could no longer hold on to its essence of "home." I felt its pain, anger, and despair. I apologized profusely and assured it that our intention was to build it back up to stronger than it had been, that our love for it was huge, and that we would all be together in it soon. I walked from room to room clearing out all of the workmen's energy and replacing it with gold, positive, healing energy. From that moment on, the house became ours in spirit and the healing and rebuilding began in earnest.

One evening I walked in and the energy was heavy and swirling. First, there was a great deal of anger, as if a parent had unleashed his fury. Then there was an underlying embarrassment, sadness, and humiliation as if a devoted child had displeased the parent he so wanted to impress. I remember saying out loud, "Wow! What happened in here?" Curious, I asked around and found out that Chris had been angry and disappointed with the subcontractors and had stern words with them. As there was a great deal of respect between the parties, the emotional reactions were quite strong.

We genuinely enjoyed the General Contractor and many of the subcontractors who worked in our home. They all commented on the good feel that our home had, and that it had been a pleasure to work in it. They said that many times that had not been the case for them at other homes.

Phyllis

While we renovated our new home, our family was between houses with no place to call home. Luckily, we were able to secure a home nearby on a short-term lease. Prior to moving into the rental, I drove over and did a little cleaning up. I walked from room to room, opening windows and taking stock of furnishings we would need, and those that would be put in storage until further notice. As I opened the window in the family room, a strong whiff of perfume surrounded me. I sensed the figure of an older woman behind me, but at ceiling height. I turned and spoke to her. I asked her what she was called. I heard, "Phyllis." Somehow I understood that Phyllis had passed away and was residing in the house, although she did not live in this house while she was alive. She had energetically resided in this house for several years and the past residents did not know she was there.

    I explained that our plan was to stay in the home for three short months and that she was welcome to stay as long as she was benevolent, as I had sensed she was. From that moment on, Phyllis took up residence in the laundry room downstairs. Our expected three months of construction timing morphed into twelve. I had time to get to know Phyllis quite well.

I never mentioned seeing a spirit in the house, but my girls flatly refused to go downstairs. The basement consisted of an open room that was piled high with boxes, a laundry room, and a windowless smaller room in which we stored excess antique dining chairs, furniture, and boxes. As all of the chairs were lined up facing forward, this smaller room was quickly nicknamed "The Church."

The Church had an energy all its own. It was dark and stuffy, and every time I entered, I repeatedly looked over my shoulder and hurried out. The entire basement felt unsettled and heavy with energy.

Phyllis never bothered anyone, but I was acutely aware of her presence in the basement. For some unknown reason, Phyllis would watch me while I was in the laundry room. While bending over the washer and dryer, my back would be to the open laundry room and doorway behind me. Phyllis' presence would be so strong I could pinpoint exactly where she was behind me and I would speak to her, albeit with goose bumps on my arms. Maybe Phyllis chose to hang out in the laundry room, as it was the only room in the basement I spent any time in. I guess we bonded by spending time together doing women's chores.

Through my beginning energy reading classes, I had learned how to read and understand energy, but I had no idea how to help a stuck soul move on. I phoned Lauren Skye for assistance. She read the energy in the basement and saw both The Church and Phyllis. Lauren described and cleared the energy in The Church. She asked Phyllis if she was ready to move on, and Phyllis said yes, but she needed help.

Lauren invited in several healing guides and said that it might take a few days for Phyllis to get the healing for issues in this life that she needed in order to continue transitioning over. For the next few days, I felt the presence of three additional spirits and Phyllis all gathered in The Church. I could sense compassionate healing taking place, with Phyllis in the center. Not wanting to intrude, I completely avoided the basement.

On the second evening, I was home by myself—just me, Phyllis, and the healing guides. I walked down the darkened hallway to the master bedroom, entered the room and saw a deceased old woman lying on my bed, as if she had been laid out in a funeral home. I wasn't frightened, probably because I instantly knew that the body was Phyllis (OK, I was a little grossed out that she was on *my* bed, but I reminded myself it was just an apparition). Standing off to one side of the room, I saw Phyllis in spirit next to one of her healing guides. Phyllis wanted me to see that I had been right all along; she had indeed once been alive, but had passed away as an older woman. She thanked me for my kindness and friendship, and for getting her the help to move on. With that, she was gone and so were all of the healing guides.

After Phyllis left us, we all noticed that things had changed in the basement. My girls were much more comfortable going downstairs and would help me with the laundry. The Church was much less foreboding and I could stay in the room longer without constantly feeling like I was intruding or being watched. As a result of experiencing Phyllis' transition, I decided that I wanted to learn how to help souls pass over.

Over the next months, as my ability to read energy and work with energy increased, Peas remained with me. Starting with the evening I saw Phyllis on my bed, Peas no longer looked like a green tornado. His appearance shifted to that of a wise older gentleman. I asked Lauren Skye why that happened. She explained that healing masters can evolve in how they are perceived and how they can be used. The fact that I did not panic when I saw Phyllis' spirit was a huge growth step. Peas saw that growth and knew that I could handle what he really looked like. He shifted his appearance to be in alignment with my abilities and his reality.

CHAPTER
4

Back to School

In time, the intuitives who had been doing energy readings for me each suggested that I get serious about taking classes so I could start answering my own questions. I finally gathered my courage and accepted their suggestions.

I took a variety of classes including Reiki, numerology, animal communication, and enrolled in a yearlong clairvoyant training course. Not only were my intuitive skills being sharpened, but I was learning more about myself and about energy as a whole. I learned that there were many aspects of energy besides using intuition to get glimpses into the past. Sometimes the information I gleaned was life changing and other times it simply reinforced what my heart knew all along.

PSYCHIC SURGEONS

In my clairvoyance training course, we learned about psychic surgeons. As healing guides, they are beings that can heal on a cellular level, resulting in physical healing. Wow, that sounds great! How do I get one?

During a guided meditation, Stacia Synnestvedt had us call in a psychic surgeon. This being was to work solely with us and in conjunction with our healing masters. I saw a large figure in front of me: his top half was a black crow and the bottom half was that of a man. I asked him what he wanted to be called and he answered, "Caw." I smiled, partly because I was not sure if that was the only sound he made, or if that was really the name he wanted. I chose the latter. I was not frightened, as there was something familiar about this figure. It was not until a few weeks later that I understood why.

The next month, Stacia led us to look at one of our own past lives. Through guided meditation, I saw a past life. I saw myself as an old woman dressed in American Indian clothing. I had been a healer, using plants and spiritual abilities to assist my fellow tribesmen. I was walking along the road with a crow at my side. When I questioned why the crow was there, I saw that the crow had once been a young man; he had been my son. Together we healed people in our tribe. My son was killed but remained with me in spirit as a crow. We continued to heal others but in a different way. He never left my side. This crow is now serving as my psychic surgeon! This crow is Caw! Welcome back, I've missed you.

Learning to Listen

In addition to taking classes, I began my own meditation practice. Every morning I tried to set aside time to be quiet, mindfully checking in with my higher self and being open to my source of energy or God.

One morning I was told in a dream that I would be studying science. The dream was extremely vivid, and the voice resonated in my thoughts when I awoke. That same morning, during meditation I heard very clearly, "sixty megahertz." OK, that's totally crazy! I don't think about science often and I wasn't even sure if megahertz was a real word, so I had no idea what sixty megahertz was all about.

I listened to this message from my guides and decided I wanted to investigate further. I looked up megahertz on the internet. I was pleased that megahertz (MHz) did exist; it is the measurement of the frequency of electromagnetic radiation. Emboldened, I looked up sixty MHz. The article that came up was regarding the relationship between the frequency of megahertz in the human body and disease (energyfanatics.com). In 1992, Bruce Tainio determined that the average frequency of a healthy human body was 62-72 MHz. Many organs from the human body were tested. The frequency of a normal brain was 72 MHz, the heart was 67-70 MHz, and the lungs were 58-65 MHz. When the body fell below the benchmark of 58 MHz, then illness and disease had the chance to set in. Colds and flu started when a body measured 57-60 MHz, receptivity to cancer began at 42 MHz, and death began at 25 MHz. In theory, bodies with a frequency above 62 MHz should not need to worry about ill health. Maybe

I was supposed to learn about helping people elevate their body's vibrational frequencies in order to maintain optimal health.

I delved further into the vibrational frequency of the human body and what could be done to prevent the body's frequency from dropping to lower levels. Suggestions included eating only fresh foods and avoiding junk food and canned or processed foods. Meditation and essential oils also increased a person's vibrational frequency.

Through faith, I learned to follow where my guides and the internet led me. As I read one article, it raised questions that led me to do more research. I relied on divine guidance to find the next article that would open up yet another topic or level of understanding. I was being led down a path of higher learning and I thoroughly enjoyed the ride.

My research on vibrational frequencies led me to look into the chakra system. The Sanskrit word chakra translates to wheel or disk, referring to spinning energy centers throughout the body. Seven main chakras align along the spine, starting from the base of the spine and continuing upwards to the crown of the head. Each chakra encompasses some part of our psychological, emotional and spiritual state of being. Each chakra represents a few specific qualities, ranging from consciousness and enlightenment in the seventh chakra, down to physical vitality and the fundamental urge to survive represented by the first chakra. As the chakra systems are well known throughout the energetic communities, a great deal of information was available online.

My study of the chakras led me to many questions: Similar to the body, did the chakras have a vibrational frequency? What were the consequences of blocked energy in the chakras? What could be done to support the wellbeing of the chakra system?

I learned a vast amount. I learned about the relationship between disease and low energy frequencies in the body and chakra systems. I learned multiple methods of healing chakras including sound therapy, meditation, light therapy, essential oils, and the use of crystals and stones. By learning how to listen to my guides I was taken on a fascinating conceptual journey I doubt I ever would have embarked on otherwise.

I realized that it would be very easy to lose myself in the research regarding energetic frequencies and decided to put that topic aside, although I was still very intrigued with this whole concept of raising a person's vibrational frequency in order to help stave off illness and disease.

A Dedicated Student

The more I was open to learning about energy, the more learning opportunities I was given. I was a sponge: reading, taking a multitude of classes, feeling, hearing, and experiencing energy on so many different levels. I had an insatiable desire to learn more and more; there was not enough time in the day to learn it all, but that wasn't going to stop me from trying!

I was embracing new skills of knowing how to read the energy of a person or place and studying how to heal others energetically. I was gingerly starting to practice working on others while assimilating and incorporating all the information I was gleaning.

As a result of all this input, I started noticing changes in myself; not only on an energetic level but on a physical level as well. My desires changed. I was no longer able to sit through what my daughter calls "shoot 'em up, kill 'em up" movies. I could not watch violent or emotionally denigrating TV programs. I was having visceral reactions to low level, negative energy including hate, bigotry, racism and prejudice.

Even my diet changed. My ability to taste foods was almost completely dulled. My taste in what I wanted to eat and could stomach became completely different. I was never a big meat eater, but now the smell and taste of meat repulsed me. My go-to foods (grains, veggies, and fruits) no longer interested me. The kinds of foods I was drawn to included corn chips, nuts, and hot water with lemon. It was hardly healthy. I was a little concerned about my health and possible stomach related issues until I heard from other intuitives that they had also experienced this phenomenon while they were going through a learning curve. As I was being emotionally and energetically healed and fine-tuned, I believe that my body was being purged as well. As a result of four months of altered dietary patterns, I lost seven pounds, which I finally put back on, once my tastes changed back to my normal pattern.

Not being much of a drinker, I went from one glass of wine a week down to zero in those four months. I had no interest in alcohol whatsoever.

I was drawn to spend my waking hours learning more and more. It felt like the only thing that mattered was the spiritual realm. Of course, I still concentrated on my family and our home, but I was not interested in the news or the typical daily life around me. I was definitely more comfortable "having my head in the clouds," as I called it, rather than my attention firmly planted in my body.

People would get into silly arguments and I could not care less. Gossip or politics? I was so not interested. I only wanted to be surrounded by higher level positive energy and my addictive relationships with my spirit guides. Where else could I go and receive unconditional love, timeless peace and quiet, and have no agenda other than my own personal growth?

My social network became teachers and intuitives who helped me learn more about the journey I was on. I had to work to find things to share with my friends who were not interested in energy work. I was able to bridge that gap by offering those friends free readings, chakra clearings, or Reiki healing work for free as I honed my skills.

Under Construction

I was driving down the street and I saw a home that was under construction. To be more precise, the front door and front alcove were the only things still in existence. Behind the first six feet of the house was a hole in the ground where the previous home had stood. How interesting! From the front of the house, one could walk by and not even notice that everything behind the front was missing.

I stopped and thought about the transformation that I had been going through on a personal level. My personal growth, including my understanding of myself as intuitive, had resulted in a major reconstruction that I was not outwardly sharing with others. I was very much like this house. On the exterior, I looked the same as I always had. Meanwhile, emotionally and philosophically, everything was under construction and I was not sure what it was going to look like when it was completed.

It made me think: how many other people do I know who are showing a familiar external facade but are in the midst of an internal reconstruction and I have no idea what they are going through?

Just Say No

I spent an entire month using my off hours to study anything and everything related to the science of energy work and spirituality. I found it fascinating and rather addicting. But where was all this leading me? I knew that I could take the path of learning more about chakra healing and vibrational frequencies, but I was not so sure it was the right path for me.

At the same time, I was insatiably taking workshops and signing up for new online programs. I dallied with the Anahata Codes, Shamanism, the Law of Attraction, and soul retrieval with the Akashic Records. Every time I signed up for a new class, I received an email invitation to learn about another author or take a different class. They all sounded interesting! I was becoming addicted to my own growth. At one point I was enrolled in six concurrent courses, some on line and some in person, and I couldn't keep up with any of them. All of these classes, while interesting, were keeping me from meditating or spending time with my guides or Divinity, the very source where I instinctively knew my real growth would be coming from. It felt like all of these distractions were now starting to hinder my growth.

I was telling a fellow intuitive about Spirit giving me too many options for continuing study. She summed it up beautifully. "Just tell them no! Tell them you have a life in a body. Then you decide what you want to learn and how you will spend your time." She explained that energy work was all about free will, including ignoring messages from Spirit, if one so chose. I did not know that I could say no. I had a lot to learn.

She was right; I had abdicated my course of action to see where Spirit would lead me. I stepped back and redefined my personal goals. As I was able to hone in on my desire of wanting to know my Divinity better, all of the other subjects started to fall by the wayside. I simply had to say no: no to multiple online classes; no to attending new workshops; no to earning yet one more certification. If my interest in these areas continued, I would have the rest of my life to delve deeper into vibrational frequencies, the Akashic Records and alchemy.

I read that we are all spiritual beings, here on earth to have a physical experience. I had to remind myself that having my head in the clouds all the time was robbing me of the physical experience I had asked for, that of being in a family, raising children, and enjoying friendships.

There were times I forced myself to put my spiritual journey on hold, in order to concentrate fully on enjoying my family. I found that no matter how long I was away from my learnings, the spiritual realm was always right there waiting for my return, as if no time had passed.

CHAPTER 5

The Teacher

In conversation with my teacher Stacia one day, I commented on the fact that everyone who was on a spiritual journey such as mine seemed to have the calling to become a teacher. She replied, "No, Ruth. Not everyone has that calling. But you do." Sigh. I saw that she was right. I don't know why, but I was being called to teach others about energy, how to acknowledge it, read it, and work with it. Through meditation, I had also been told repeatedly that I should start writing a blog about my experiences.

Writing a Blog

One morning while meditating, I heard that I was supposed to write a "blog." What's a blog? Isn't that something that young people do on the internet? I had never even seen a blog.

Why would I be writing a blog? Because I was going to share with other people all the things I'd been learning. So now I had to learn not only what a blog was, but how to write one. I enlisted my technology advisor, my twelve-year-old, to help me go about setting up and putting together a blog. And I started writing. When I completed one blog entry, another popped into my mind. If I didn't write it down right away, it was gone as quickly as it came. I wasn't sure where the ideas or words were coming from, but I resonated with each message, so it was OK. Sometimes the vignettes were creative, other times, more personal. Each blog was instructional in nature. Someone was guiding me to become a teacher. I'm not sure the words were all my own thoughts; but I agreed with the message, so I wrote it!

Sensing Energy

How do you sense energy? Do you hear it, see it, feel it, or just know it? When I get information, sometimes I can see it as if I was seeing it with my eyes. Sometimes I feel it, and when I feel it sometimes I can actually feel the pain or emotions, the anxiousness, the rapid heart rate of someone going through a difficult experience or an illness.

Knowingness, or just knowing that what you are sensing is real, has a different feeling to it. It's hard to explain, but there is an absolute assuredness. Sometimes I get to hear things when energy is trying to get a point across. The other day, while providing Reiki to a friend, I kept hearing the word "menopause." When I asked her if she had been having difficulties with menopause, her eyes stared straight into mine and she asked "Why?" and then she gave me a big smile. Her energy was telling me its story. It ends up that she had been frustrated dealing with her symptoms of menopause and had just gotten off the phone with her doctor. She was shocked that I was able to get the message of what was bothering her without her telling me in words.

I have even had the opportunity to be able to smell places and things that I've experienced energetically. It really drives the point home to me that am somehow being transported to a different place and time that was very real for someone else.

So how do *you* sense energy? Stop and listen the next time you feel compelled to pay attention to the energy nearby. You don't need to question its validity and you don't have to question your own sanity. Energy exists and some people are able to sense it better than others. If you are one of those people that sense energy on a regular basis, there are others like you. Sometimes it is a comfort to connect with other people that know, understand, and appreciate what you are experiencing.

The Aha Moments

What is it that makes one moment in time so different from any other moment? What is it that sends you energetic or spiritual messages of knowingness about somebody else? Do you run from those moments, shut down, and turn inward while trying not to notice? Or do you open your attention, smile, and realize that this is a message meant specifically for you? Sometimes life gives us what I call "aha moments." Aha moments are those moments when you have received an energetic message and you figure out what it means. Sometimes it's confusing knowing what the message is and what you're supposed to get from it. Sometimes I need to just sit and contemplate it and ask myself, "Why am I feeling this; are these even my emotions?"

When I stop and take the time to figure out where that immediate sense of dread or sadness came from, I can usually figure out where I picked up that energy signal.

Are you learning to trust those aha moments? Are you learning not to run, but to stop and embrace the moment that has been given to you?

If you have received an aha moment and need someone to help you figure out what its importance is, there are others like you that are open to reading and understanding energy. I encourage you to create a community of like-minded souls that are open to discussing and helping to interpret what those hits of energy mean for you. The more you pay attention and listen to those aha moments, the more of them you will have and the sooner you will see that you are being guided on a journey: not just any journey, but your own personal journey. If you are interested in following your soul path, stop and listen to the aha moments.

You've Got Mail!

How do you know when you are getting an energetic or spiritual message, or what I like to call a "hit" or a "ping"? Sometimes I get a tingly feeling in my heart (fourth) chakra or my solar plexus (third) chakra.

I have learned to trust that ping. If at all possible, I will then stop what I am doing and wait for a message. Sometimes on the physical plane, it means I will soon be receiving a text or an email about something I have been working on energetically. Sometimes, I will get the answer through meditation or prayer.

Be aware of your body and when it is receiving a signal that you have an incoming energetic or spiritual message. You never know when you've got mail!

Symbolism

Some days, everything I look at is really just exactly what it seems. But there are some days that the things I look at are actually telling me a story about something else. With energy and spiritual work, I find that symbolism and metaphors are often used for teaching lessons or imparting knowledge.

For example, I was enjoying a glass of chocolate milk and chai the other morning. I grabbed the glass and it fell about an inch onto the granite countertop and shattered. Milk, chai, ice, and glass were all over the counter and floor, liquid dripping down the cabinets. It was a spectacular mess! How could that huge mess happen from a glass falling one inch? It must have hit just right. As I rarely spill things and am not particularly accident prone, I asked myself if there was some symbolism I should pay attention to? My mind thought of "don't cry over spilled milk." I didn't feel any connection to that, so I was quiet for a minute and waited for the symbolism to come to me. I heard "it doesn't require a lot of effort to make a spectacular impact on the world!" Ahhhh, I can resonate with that!

Validation

Why is it that some days I need so much validation? Am I really seeing all of these images? Is this all crazy? Am I losing it? So many times, I have sought validation. And each time, it has come to me!

My sister-in-law Sharon was in town and she had a tight, painful knot between her shoulders. I offered a Reiki treatment and she accepted. Two weeks later she sent me a lovely card thanking me for the treatment and letting me know that she was still free from the pain in her back. It was so validating to receive a written affirmation that the Reiki was effective. I truly can make a difference. I can facilitate healing with my guides. This is real. I will keep Sharon's card as a reminder when I feel a need for validation.

My need for validation has gotten less as I am able to validate myself, and Spirit is always there to validate me as well. I believe in me. I believe in this journey. I believe in energy and I believe in divine guidance. I have everything I need for my own validation.

PENNIES FROM HEAVEN

September 1, 2005, the morning my much-loved mother-in-law, Helen, passed away, our extended family decided to meet at our home for breakfast. Totally devastated at losing Mom, I left hospice and headed home. As I walked to our front door, the bush to the left of our door was covered in beautiful yellow butterflies! I had never seen so many butterflies gathered in one place. What a beautiful gift of love and connection to Mom in Spirit.

About six months later, I was upstairs with my daughters, looking at Mom's fabrics. Helen loved doing hand crafts, and we brought a great many of her fabrics home. As we sorted the fabrics, we laughed while remembering many of the things that we loved and missed about Grandma. My eye happened to go to the window, and hovering outside, by the second story window was a beautiful yellow butterfly. Aw, thank you for this moment of love and healing!

I equate certain symbols with people I love that have passed on. As Helen sends butterflies, Sylvia's husband Cliff sends dragonflies. My father-in-law, Bob, brings wind shaking through aspen leaves, or "Quakies," as he called them.

My dear friend Sylvia sends coins. Shortly after her death, she sent dimes. I was finding dimes daily for the first two months after she passed. Apparently, inflation has struck everywhere, and now she simply leaves me pennies or nickels. It is all good. Since Sylvia passed away three and a half years ago, I have found four dollar bills and 274 coins of varying denominations. I just have to believe that this is above the typical daily average! Finding a coin brings a smile to my face, a tear to my eye, and helps me to remember Sylvia and the connection that we still share.

Stay Grounded

One morning, my youngest daughter was in a terrible funk. Her frustration and anger soon wore me down and I allowed myself to become grumpy as well. I finally couldn't stand the angst anymore and retreated to go make sure that I was grounded, so the rest of our day could be civil. Imagine my surprise when I realized that my youngest daughter, my husband, my other daughter, and our three dogs were all grounding themselves through me. I very quickly removed them from my personal energy and immediately felt more stable and less anxious.

I considered why my family might be feeling the need to ground through me and realized that the mass shooting in Orlando was just the day before. I think we are all internalizing violence and the political climate across the country in our own way.

In these very uncertain times, hold onto those truths that are most important to you. Surround yourself with love, stay grounded, and open your heart and mind to your God or your experience of the Divine. Stay focused on higher vibrational energy and be a clear channel for your Higher Truth to spread light and love to those around you.

Embrace Your Inner Crone

The months leading up to my fiftieth birthday were somewhat traumatic; in fact, I faced the day white-knuckled, kicking and screaming, with an impending sense of dread. Turning fifty-five, by contrast, was effortless and inviting. What had happened in those years to calm my inner angst?

Three years ago, I began my journey to understand and embrace Spirit, clairvoyance, and healing. As a result of this inner work, I have been able to embrace my past, recognize familial and cultural programming, and let go of energy and emotions that were not mine to own. I have shifted my (albeit Americanized) perceptions about aging, and have come to respect wisdom with experience: my own wisdom built on trial and error and many years of experience.

I have breakfast once a week with my also-retired colleagues, whom I have come to know and love over the years. I look around the table and I do not look for evidence of physical aging, rather, I see a combined commitment of more than 120 years at the worksite, all with the intent of making the lives of others more manageable. I sit with Helen, Jean, and Constance, and I see, a political activist, an artist and a social worker. Our conversations are rich with personal introspection, current events, political musings, concern for loved ones, and support for each other. Each week, I give myself the rich gift of basking in friendship and steeping in heartfelt conversations.

If given the chance to be ten years younger, I would never go back. The inner peace and wisdom I have gained by knowing Spirit came at the same time as some wrinkles were forming. I look in the mirror and see a woman who has gained in inner value and proudly earned each of her years.

I have learned to embrace the term "crone" for myself. Not the ugly, ill-tempered crone as sometimes portrayed in fairy tales. But the wise, comfortable in her skin, old soul who can share compassion as well as counsel, and who doesn't have to look a certain way in order to feel OK about herself.

From the Garden

I have always enjoyed Mother's Day because it marks the beginning of longer days and spring planting. I love going to the greenhouse to feel the warm, moist air and to see the new plants come in. I always buy more than I have the energy to plant; there is something about the smell of the soil, the bright green of the foliage, and the promise of flowering buds that I just can't resist.

As I was digging holes for purple clematis and Japanese honeysuckle, I was working in an area of the garden that was already highly saturated with water. The soil was compact and had the consistency of very wet clay rather than loose, inviting soil. Tired of digging in clay and in my desire to get the plants into the ground quickly, I made the hole just large enough for the plant to fit, knowing full well that the recommended space should be two times the size of the pot. I really do understand that the roots need space, good soil, and proper drainage in order to not just survive, but thrive. I hoped against hope that these new plants would be able to make the most of this unwelcoming environment and grow strong with amazing flowers.

Shortly afterward, as I was thinking about my own spiritual growth, I saw a vision of my new clematis trying to create a home in an unwelcome, too small, already saturated area and I wondered if that was what I was doing to my soul's growth as well. Did I create such a complicated, busy lifestyle that I was trying to shoehorn meditation time into the too small, already saturated space that I had set aside? Was I spending so much time trying to create my spiritual/energetic business that I was taking my emphasis off the things that mattered most, namely my family and my own spiritual growth?

In my desire to know everything immediately, I was dabbling in several different courses, spending valuable time spreading my attention much too thinly. Were these courses anything more than distractions or weeds in my garden, choking out the healthy plants of spiritual growth? I brought these concerns up during meditation and I heard an answer loud and clear: "Not every class is worth your time." OK, I got it!

It was time for me to either sleep less, or re-evaluate the complexities that I call life and make some changes. It was time to drain the bog of excess energy and ideas that were pooling in my brain. It was time to turn over the soil, take a deep breath, be still, and nourish that part of me that is open and accepting to Spirit and Spirit's stories and lessons.

CHAPTER 6

Enter the Divine

The year-long clairvoyant training course I was taking was winding down, with only two months more to go. I was hoping by that point in time I would have more answers than questions. But this didn't seem to be the case. What was this journey of learning I was being taken on? Where would it lead? When would it end? I sensed that instead of things winding down for me energetically, it was time to fasten my seat belt.

I completed a Usui Reiki 1 course online and loved it! Reiki is a traditional Japanese energetic healing form. I had heard that sometimes a Reiki attunement (an initiation ritual) may result in receiving a spirit guide. Guides that accompany Reiki are thought to be of the highest frequencies and vibrations, which was important to me. Some Reiki practitioners have the same guides each time they facilitate Reiki, while others have different guides at different times.

While I had a healing master and psychic surgeon, I had not received a spirit guide with my Reiki 1 course. I was very disappointed. Did that mean that I was doing something wrong? That I wasn't worthy? That Reiki must be taught in person and not on-line? That Reiki was a bunch of hooey? I was fearful of what a spirit guide might look like, and I was not sure if I even wanted one. What if they were frightening or evil? How would I know if they were of high frequencies, low level vibrations or just a bad match for me? Even with all of my reservations, I was somehow still hopeful that I would eventually receive another spirit guide.

Good Things Come in Threes

After Reiki 1, I tried a "Reiki for Animals" course online. Every Saturday morning for four weeks, I sequestered myself and listened in while my teacher, Nancy Windheart, led class via tele-conference call. During the second class, Nancy led us in meditation. During the quiet, I felt loving Divine energy behind me; not a little, but a lot! I knew the high vibrational frequency was associated with God and white healing light and I was not afraid.

Excitedly, I turned around to see what energetic presence was behind me. I was given the profound gift of three spiritual beings representing Reiki, the Divine Mother, and Jesus Christ! WHOA!! I was totally humbled and awestruck! I burst into tears with profound awe and gratitude.

Reiki is a highly effective form of energetic healing that can be used over time and across distances. Reiki is brought in through the practitioner's hands and directed toward the recipient. Reiki can provide a blanket-like calm to a situation, can clear home or business energy, and can provide physical, emotional, and energetic healing. The spiritual being representing Reiki was a masculine presence and said I could refer to him as "Reiki." Albeit not a "Divine" figure by my definition, Reiki is a highly gifted healer.

I had not known Divine Mother prior to that morning, but I recognized her immediately. Divine Mother is the essence of all things compassion, nurturing, and maternal. Some people call her Mother Earth; some see her as Mary, the Divine mother of Jesus Christ. Divine Mother encompasses nature, heaven, and earth. She brings an all-embracing, all-consuming love to her healing.

I have no words to describe the impact of having the presence of Jesus right behind me! I grew up in the Methodist church. Literally. It was across the street from my childhood home. Being a latchkey kid, I stopped there daily after school and checked in with the church secretary on my way home. My first paid job was to clean the sanctuary pews of used tissues and old church bulletins, getting it ready for the next Sunday. I received ten cents each Wednesday for my trouble.

Thanks to my oldest brother, I had a life changing experience while in Junior High, where I was first introduced to Jesus Christ. After that, I taught Sunday School and performed in our church's youth singing group for five years. My faith, whether spoken out loud or not, kept me out of trouble, and served as a cornerstone of my personality, morals, and, I believe, soul. As Caroline, one of my fellow clairvoyant students said to me during a reading of my soul's purpose, "Do you even know how religious you are?" Yep, I think I do.

By seeing Jesus Christ during the Reiki meditation, I received the validation that my involvement in Reiki was acceptable in God's eyes, which was incredibly important to me. I realized that this Reiki stuff was real, and it came with an amazing support system! I later read that Christ often shows up as a spirit guide for Christian Reiki practitioners.

That was the only time I was visited by Jesus. About two months later while in meditation, a spirit guide came to me as a non-denominational healer. He appeared as a short man wearing black priest pants and shirt with a white tab collar. I thought, OK, he's Catholic. I asked him what he wanted me to call him. I heard the name "Rabbi." Umm, what? I then realized that he was a holy man, but not of any denomination as we know it. Together we agreed on the name, "Man of God."

Shortly after that, during one of my clairvoyant courses, we were taught how to use a healing energy called Christ-Force. The energy felt like clear white light overlaid with pure acceptance, compassion, and love. I was really pleased to experience Christ-Force! I appreciated that my teacher and her teachers recognized and accepted the healing power of Jesus Christ. After learning to use Christ-Force, I was joined by a male healing being that came to me wheeling a wheelbarrow with a crucifix in it. He chose to be called "Christ-Force" and heals using Christ-Force energy.

I readily accepted both Man of God and Christ-Force as representatives of my religious faith. I have called on these spirit or healing guides frequently and they always come as soon as I request their presence. I have personally experienced their healing powers, and I have used their energy to assist in the energetic healing and clearings for friends and animals.

In Search of Angels

Browsing through the Internet for things energy-related, I would often run across articles that had to do with angels. When I would look at the items they were selling, they were typically female angels dressed very voluptuously and I really wondered what this craze was all about. Clearly this had to be some sort of gimmick, geared strictly for males, or something designed just to make money.

Growing up Methodist, we really were not exposed to many stories about angels. There was an angel at Jesus's birth and there was an angel at the tomb when the women went and found that Jesus had risen from the dead. Angels were never personal; they never visited you or taught you. I had never experienced anything to do with an angel and I could not imagine that I would embrace any of these voluptuous vixens into my existence. I had gotten to the point of disappointedly renouncing that there was no such thing as an angel.

The day after I made this sad, personal proclamation, I was at one of my clairvoyant classes. During the lesson, we were in meditation, receiving a healing. A very large, very white presence entered my meditative space. Curious, I tried to figure out what it was. I was able to see some sort of ridges; looking closer I was astonished to see that what I thought were ridges were actually feathers! I was looking up close at the back side of an angel wing! It was not any voluptuous vixen but a very large-winged, male energy, with immense strength, power, and light. I asked this dove-angel what he liked to be called, and I heard, "Michael." As soon as I acknowledged that I understood he was an angel, he flew off with such power that I could feel the air whoosh around me! I was very quick to take back my proclamation that there was no such thing as an angel. I was personally pleased that there were such beings and immensely touched that one cared enough to come show me that I had been wrong.

I soon realized that my dove-angel Michael was actually Archangel Michael! Michael, whose name means "Who is Like God," is the most well-known angel and is found in the sacred texts of Judaism, Christianity, and Islam. Michael is known as the overseer of the archangels, and for fighting against evil with the power of good. Michael is an exceptionally strong angel who protects and defends people who love God. Archangel Michael is very large; has immense power, strength, and light; and serves to help people in times of crisis, as well as help souls to pass on. Archangel Michael has shown me many things; he has a sense of humor and wonder, and is an amazing teacher.

Since that day, I have been so fortunate to get to spend time with some of the other archangels. I have had the pleasure of being in the presence of archangels Gabriel and Raphael. Archangel Gabriel is the famous angel from the Bible who told Mary of the impending birth of her son, Jesus. Some see Gabriel as male, some female. I see her as female. Gabriel, whose name means "God is my Strength," is a muse for writers, artists, and communicators, motivating them to overcome fear and procrastination. She is very clever, very creative, and very inspiring. Time spent with her results in things like downloads of children's books in my head and immense motivation to write. She is clear in giving directions that I can understand, loving, supportive, and always makes me feel capable of writing something that others might want to read.

Archangel Raphael, whose name means "God Heals," is also an archangel of Judaism, Christianity, and Islam. In the Christian tradition, Raphael is generally associated with the angel mentioned in the Gospel of John as stirring the water at the healing pool of Bethesda. Archangel Raphael is a healer, very strong and very masculine. He is a true teacher and has taken me on spiritual journeys in order to increase my knowledge as a student and healer. I have called on him for assistance with healing and he has never disappointed me.

The archangels I have seen are of the light, strong, loving, and pure. There has been no question in my mind that they are the real deal. I have also seen many smaller and seemingly less powerful angels. They are also white, of the light, and have been in a position of service to others. If you desire to feel the presence of an angel, I firmly believe in setting your intention and asking your God, Source, or Divine Spirit for an introduction. And then wait for divine timing. I hope that your time with angels will be as profound and life changing as what I have been fortunate to experience!

Junior

It was spring break and our family was on vacation. We rented a home that ended up being right next door to a small graveyard. The garage separated our front yard from the cemetery and was approximately ten feet from a row of old, worn headstones and graves. Our twelve-year-old was more than just a little freaked out over our new neighbors.

One morning at two AM, I was awakened by what sounded like drag racing in front of our house. I fell back asleep but a little later I was woken by flashing lights outside my window. I didn't think too much about it until the next morning when I saw there had been a serious accident right outside our front door.

A gold pick-up truck sat in a crumpled heap in the graveyard; three of its tires dug into the ground as if it had spun in a circle pushing its way into the soft earth. The front windshield and driver's side window were shattered, the airbag deployed, and there was significant damage to three sides of the truck including the driver's door. The truck had missed the garage of our rental house by less than a foot.

Over the next few days, my energetic attention kept being pulled toward the accident. Who was the driver, what were the circumstances, and did the driver live to tell about it? My intuition was telling me no, he did not, yet Spirit kept goading me to seek answers.

Finally, my intuitive questions were answered. I was shown that the driver of the truck had been killed. I saw that he left a companion and a toddler-age daughter. I got the message that everyone called him Junior, except for the mother of his daughter. She was the only one that believed in him, took him seriously as an adult, and called him by his first name. Junior was considered to be a troublemaker and no one ever expected much of him. He had a way of messing things up, being in the wrong place at the wrong time, and this was yet another example of that.

Spiritually, I was called out next door to the graveyard. In my mind's eye I went out and saw Junior sitting on the curb, his head in his hands. He was talking about how he always messed things up. I believe that he had died so quickly in the crash that his spirit was not aware that he had passed away. I sat with him for a while and was surprised that I was not afraid. I was actually quite calm. One of my spirit guides, Divine Mother, joined us and I moved out of the way. She gave Junior a healing and then left with him by her side. I believe she was helping him to move on spiritually.

That night I realized that I was shown this experience for a reason; our ability to book this particular rental house right next to the graveyard where the accident happened was probably not a coincidence. I realized that I could be instrumental on a spiritual level by helping souls that had left their physical body to transition and pass on.

Being in a remote area, Junior's truck sat in the graveyard for four days before it was towed. Our friend went to take a closer look the morning it was taken away. He came back and said, "Oh, how sad. There was a child's sippy cup in the front seat." Somehow, I had already known that.

The Dove

One morning shortly after seeing Junior, I woke up after having a vivid dream. I dreamt that I was holding an injured bird. I put my hands on it and felt that it had a broken neck. With my newfound confidence as a healer, I expected that I would see myself healing it. I felt an energetic reaction between my hands and the bird. Then the dove's soul flew out and I saw that the bird was dead. I was stunned. Then I saw that helping a soul transition to the next life is as much a service as healing them physically.

CHAPTER
7

Animal Communication

Even as a young girl, I wanted to be able to communicate with animals. Reiki for Animals and other animal communication courses taught me how to communicate with animals and assist with their healing. I love to be able to read the energy of animals!

Just for fun, I extrapolated these same skills to communicate with insects. I have been able to persuade ants and wasps to move out of a given area by communicating spirit to spirit with them. Yes, insects have spirits! What a delicious gift I gave to myself by developing these skills!

Noah's Ark

Several times during readings, I have been told that I am surrounded by animal guides. Nothing could make me happier or fill my heart with more love and joy. I have enjoyed the company of animal spirit doves, bears, rabbits, elk, gazelle, geese, goats, squirrels, a turkey, a porcupine, a skunk, and a camel. I often look up the different meanings of the animal spirit guides online and thoroughly enjoy looking for the story behind the symbolism.

Our house pets in bodies like to communicate with me spirit to spirit. Currently our home is shared with hamsters, fish, a Diamond dove, a hermit crab and three dogs. Maddie, our cavapoo puppy, enjoys showing up in spirit during my clairvoyant classes and often sits very close by when I am giving someone a reading or healing. I completed a past life reading on Maddie and saw her as a baby bunny in a hutch outside our front door, four years ago. The hutch and the bunny family were destroyed by a skunk. During Maddie's past life reading, I saw the skunk from the baby bunny's vantage, and felt her panic during the life and death struggle. Apparently, the bunny wanted to be part of our family and came back to us via Maddie.

Tucker, our fourteen-year-old cockapoo, is constantly seeking me out for reassurance and love. Although he has dealt with back pain and cancer, he is very clear to point out that he has no intention of going anywhere any time soon. As the patriarch of our dog family, he holds court and lets me know if he thinks I have done something wrong, like when I feed the other two dogs first. He gets totally annoyed when Maddie plays ball too close to him, although he has shared with me that sometimes he actually thinks she is pretty silly.

Jack, our twelve-year-old cockapoo, suffers from anxiety and middle child syndrome. He complained vehemently when we brought Maddie into our family. He would say to me, "You just don't know how annoying she is!" Sometimes Jack will show up with Maddie in spirit at my class. When he does, he smiles like it is the funniest thing that he can join me across town. He enjoys our inside joke and is happy and upbeat when I get back home.

When Lola, our Diamond dove, lost her partner Sparky, we thought that she was going to starve herself to death. Spirit to spirit I asked her why she was hanging on. She showed me that she needed to stay with me so I could move further with animal communication, and that I needed to believe in myself. She was afraid that if she was not here to keep me moving forward, I might just give it up all together. I believe that she was correct.

Kumu is a deep blue Betta fish named after my dear friend Sylvia, whose license plate read KUMU (Hawaiian for teacher). Kumu encourages me to do animal readings and energetically flips like crazy whenever I ask him for advice about my future as an animal communicator. What he lacks in vocabulary he makes up for with exuberance. He is one of my strongest animal supporters. Funny, we have had many Bettas come through our doors, mostly as short-timers, but Kumu has such a strong soul and sense of self. I hope he is around for a long, long time to come.

Last summer I enjoyed taking the girls to the farm where goats were milked by volunteers on a daily basis.

We enjoyed our time with the goats and I was particularly amused when Clover, one of the goats joined me in spirit during my clairvoyant classes. What a treat to have an unexpected visitor!

Goose Talk

My Reiki for Animals teacher, Nancy Windheart, announced that we needed to find a wild animal on which to practice Reiki. I will let you think about that for a minute. Where was I supposed to find a wild animal that would be willing to sit still *and* give me permission to do a Reiki treatment?

While I could get the occasional squirrel to stop and look at me, I could not entice them to stay. Time was running out and I did not want to crawl back to class not having completed my homework. So, I turned to my backyard. We are very fortunate to live near a lake that is on a migration path for Canadian geese. On any given day during the winter, we can see and hear hundreds of geese as they stop to rest and then take off again heading south before nightfall. But, would any goose be willing to let me work on him?

Out of desperation, I plopped down in my living room, asked Reiki to assist in bringing a wild animal close to me, and waited. Nearly an hour later, about twenty geese flew in and foraged for food near our fence. Normally the geese stay closer to the lake, so I was seeing this as a positive sign! From the comfort of my home, I thanked Reiki, put my hands in a position to serve as a conduit for the healing energy and asked the geese if any of them would accept a Reiki healing. One of the geese looked at me and didn't budge. That was my bird!

As he was receiving Reiki, I took the opportunity to read his energy. He had a very strong, earthy, oily, almost nutty essence to his energy. I was reminded of the comparison between wild rice and white rice. As a pescatarian, I appreciate the awkwardness and morbid humor in describing a goose's energy using the words nutty, earthy, and oily.

Another goose came close to my "Reikified" friend. My goose squawked, spread his wings, and loudly charged at him. Like a true mother, I responded, "Did you really need to respond that strongly? Wasn't that a bit much?" My goose replied, "Yeah, but you don't know him! He always does things like that!"

I was so grateful to Nancy, for providing this amazing opportunity to experience wildlife from another vantage.

MATCHING PICTURES

I meditate first thing every morning, while the rest of my family sleeps. What a beautiful way to check in with my spirit guides, ground myself, and get a fresh start to each day. One morning, I posed a recurring question to my guides: I know I am to be writing, but I just don't know where all of this is heading. I don't know what to do. At that very moment, Maddie, the puppy, barked to be let outside. I walked her outside across the backyard.

Back by the lake, I saw a goose pop its head up and stare directly at me. She wasn't afraid, and was very intent; she seemed to be looking right through me. Very few of the Canadian geese were still in town, most having already continued their journey. Any left would have been staying back with an injured or ill companion, waiting either for a recovery or a death.

I did not see any other geese around. Why was this goose here? And why was she all alone? I immediately understood as I heard and felt: "I lost my partner. I am alone. I don't know what to do." I immediately sent my answer: "You are safe here. Stay as long as you need." However, I could not imagine this lone goose staying here by itself over the coming summer. Did I really think that she would be safe here?

As a true mother and teacher, I started brainstorming on her behalf. I said, "You can wait for another goose, which might take a really long time (I am thinking months), or you can start flying. You actually know what to do. Trust yourself."

The goose and I had a stare down for about 30 more seconds. Then she let out a few hopeful goose honks, stretched and flapped her wings, and then took off toward the south. I smiled and thought, "That's my girl!"

Then it hit me. I also knew what to do. I headed back into the house and started writing.

I've Got It!

After living with us for two years, my daughter's hamster, Maui, died of old age. Now, somehow there was a hamster size void in *my* heart. Seriously? I couldn't believe it!

At the pet store, we found four hamster brothers all together in one cage. My daughter asked me to read them, and two of them had very sweet personalities and seemed like a good fit for our family. Frederick was all brown, very lively, sure of himself, and liked to communicate. The other, Sundae, had a sweet demeanor, was timid in spirit, and was seeking a connection with others. Sundae was white with dark brown splotches and looked like vanilla ice cream with chocolate sauce drizzled on him.

We brought the hamsters home and Frederick eagerly explored his new surroundings. Sundae, on the other hand, looked like he was in shock. I put my hand on his cage, spoke to him, and asked Reiki to ease his transition. Sundae snuggled in the corner next to my hand and lay quietly. I thought his reaction extremely odd, but it reinforced my belief that he was seeking connection with others. Later that night, Sundae came to me in spirit and sat cuddled up just below my left shoulder and was very frightened. I told him he could stay with me in spirit and I would keep him safe. I figured there was a reason that my hamster-sized void was filled with this particular hamster.

The next morning, my daughter was playing with Sundae on the bathroom floor. She had carefully covered up a small crack between the door and the tile floor, as she didn't want Sundae to make an escape. She did not know, however, about the hole at the base of the bathroom cabinet. Sundae promptly found it, followed his hamster instincts, and quickly got himself wedged between the cabinet and the drywall. Of course, we had no way of seeing him or being able to retrieve him.

As we had to leave for school, we left Sundae in his dark cabinet jail and left a trail of treats leading back to his open cage. In the late afternoon, we came back home, but Sundae was nowhere to be seen. I began in earnest to try to locate him with the hopes that he had not travelled behind the drywall into parts unknown. As it was still light out and hamsters are nocturnal, I figured we would not hear of Sundae's whereabouts until approximately ten o'clock that night.

In desperation, I sat in the bathroom and silently called upon Reiki and Divine Mother for healing of this precarious situation. The last thing we wanted was for Sundae to perish within the walls of our home, only to be found later via the smell of decaying hamster.

As I was calling on my guides for help, I heard scuffling and gnawing behind the cabinet! Sundae had woken up and I was able to pinpoint his exact location. Through the use of mirrors and flashlights, I was able to ascertain that Sundae was wedged in an area about one and a half inches wide by two feet deep. I was able to see that he was trying to jump out of the same hole that he had gotten himself into and that he was not able to do so.

Enter Wayne and the power tools. As holes were being drilled through the wood cove base to enlarge the hole for Sundae to escape, the sound of the electric drill was deafening. I could feel Sundae in spirit huddled up against my chest completely frightened. If a hamster's spirit could scream, I was feeling it. Out of desperation, I called out again to Reiki asking for energetic healing for the situation. I asked for what I call "Reiki Calm" for Sundae while the drilling was going on, as I was worried about his heart failing from the stress and the noise. I personally began to feel a slight sense of calm.

I continued to agitatedly plead with Reiki; I explained

that Sundae had come into our family for a reason less than twenty-four hours prior and that it was just wrong that this particular animal should be trapped with our being unable to save it.

I very clearly heard the words, "I've got it!" And no, the voice wasn't from my husband! I understood. Stand down, Ruth! I realized that if I had listened to the calming energy I was receiving, I would have understood that Reiki was already in play and was making sure that things were moving forward in order to rescue Sundae.

Wayne finished drilling the escape hatch for Sundae. I was able to finally see the little hamster in his entirety. He had been sitting about three inches from where the extremely loud drilling was taking place and he looked like he was in the deepest sleep. I watched him breathe; at first I was afraid that he was in shock and dehydrated from being in the cupboard all day. I then got the sense that he had, in fact, been protected by Reiki, and had slept through the loud drilling. Now that's what I call Reiki Calm.

Now it was up to Sundae to squeeze his way out to freedom. My daughter's friend lured him out with a fresh strawberry and was able to get a hold of him and secure him in his cage.

Lesson for my daughter: never play with the hamster on the floor.

Lesson for me: when you ask for guidance from Divine Mother and Reiki and you feel the sense of calm, trust in that and believe that they've got things covered.

CHAPTER
8

One Love

In hindsight, I can see that I was being prepared for Open Clinic, a place on the spiritual realm where souls, with and without bodies, could come for healing. During meditation in late February 2016, I was energetically escorted and taken up through our blue sky, out of our atmosphere, and into the black of the universe. I had no fear and knew that at any moment I could come back and ground myself. I was taken to experience an incredibly bright, white light, so white that mere words cannot describe it. I was told that it was "One Love." I wanted desperately to understand more, but I was brought back to my physical plane. Each day I was shown and taught a little more.

ONE LOVE

    Looking back on it, an entire month was spent teaching me about One Love. During meditation, I would be energetically escorted and I would float upwards and into One Love. Each time I went, I was automatically very energized, yet at the same time, at peace. I felt such calm, unconditional love, and a sense that all was right in my body and in the world. Frankly, there were times I just wanted to stay and not come back to the reality of my life in this physical world.

    I was hungry to understand what I was experiencing. While with One Love, I felt like I was having my own personal communication with God. It must be God, because nothing else could be so all-encompassing, accepting, or loving.

    I wanted to have words to describe it. I heard the words: "One Planet. One God." I wrestled with, but understood, that there really is only one God, regardless of the religious delineations and titles (Catholic, Baptist, etc.) that man has created in the name of religion. I saw that all of the different religious groups that worship a loving God are in fact "gateway religions." They are all worshipping one power, one force, one God.

I saw that One Love is the all-encompassing God, Source, or Divinity of Open Clinic.

ON THE MOUNTAIN

During late February, I completed a Reiki 2 course. During the Reiki attunement, a form of initiation, I took an energetic journey to a mountaintop and saw my higher self for the first time. She was tall, looked to be in her late twenties to mid-thirties with long, blond, flowing curls. My higher self, later named Mi, (sounds like "Me," but spelled fancier) went to all of the places instructed by my Reiki Master. At the end of the attunement, Mi entered a large field and was met by hundreds or thousands of souls. I understood that I was now a member of this community of souls. Interestingly, another member of my Reiki class had the exact same images of joining the larger community during her attunement.

The next morning, I meditated and was taken back up to the mountaintop where the attunement had taken place. I asked about all of the souls I had encountered and asked if they had all also been through the Reiki attunement? I heard, "All these souls know One Love."

A week or so later, during mediation, I was escorted to where nonhuman (alien) life forms enter our atmosphere. I saw that there are other universes and that there are people on Earth who originated from other universes. They showed me that the aliens or "others" were capable of connecting with humans, but it felt different than how we know and understand love. I heard that the others in human form need to be taught what our version of love looks like to fit in unnoticed. I saw that they did not connect with One Love (I still have questions about all this, but am merely reporting what I was shown). I was then taken to One Love back in our universe for a beautiful, energizing chakra healing.

A month later, I was energetically escorted to One Love. I received a physical healing on my sinuses. I experienced immense joy and was surrounded by warmth, comfort, and love. I was pleased to see that One Love can do physical healing.

During meditation, I was flown back to the mountaintop and I saw that the same souls from my Reiki attunement were there. The words "One Love" were mentioned and from overhead I saw everyone cheering and jumping for joy. I was surprised to see that my Higher Self was included in the revelry! It was clear that we all had experienced, believed in, and loved the same energy.

Guiding Principles

I was given the following tenets of One Love:

- One Love is of God.
- I can access One Love by myself. I can go there.
- A person is taken spiritually or energetically up to One Love.
- One Love healing energy can be brought down to a person.
- One Love may be brought down and used on many people at one time.
- One Love cannot do harm.
- One Love may be used on someone without their express permission. Meaning, if there is a natural or manmade disaster, a person can provide One

Love healing to an individual or the masses without express permission. Each person will receive only the healing that their spirit is open to accepting.
- If someone shows up spiritually, I may assume that they want the healing from One Love.
- Souls and people will be able to experience One Love without my taking them there.

I was escorted energetically out into the universe on a timeline of my life. I was taken out to before my time and told that my soul's purpose, which I had signed up for, was to write and educate about One Love. One Love is of God. I am to teach and heal using One Love.

Mount Chakra

When I am shown something by Spirit, I have many questions about what I am seeing, and I tend to ask a lot of questions. Sometimes I get clear answers and sometimes I don't. I had a lot of questions about One Love. In response, I was shown an area of One Love up close and personal. I found myself in a white mist of One Love.

Thinking that I would not be able to hold One Love directly because it would be too intense, I set out to find crystals or a stone that would be able to hold the healing frequency. I wanted to be able to carry home the creamy, bright white healing energy. I looked online for a stone that was opaque, yet creamy white. Nothing stood out to me.

As if being rewarded for being a dedicated student, once I looked up opaque white stones on the internet, my lessons during meditation went to a whole new level. Like a zoom lens on a camera, my ability to focus on the white healing space went from fuzzy white to a clear image of a huge white crystallized wall directly in front of me. It reminded me of a white quartz rock with all of the lines and fissures.

This wall of white healing energy was immense. There was no definable end in sight in any direction. I saw no sky, no horizon, just this massive, crystallized white mass.

My month-long obsession with studying scientific principles of energy was finally becoming useful. I recalled reading online about crystals being able to retain healing frequencies. I knew in One Love, I was looking at some form of crystals that contained healing frequencies. I didn't know much about crystals, but if the healing energy of One Love is in a crystal-like material, I wondered if it could be stored in a similar crystal material. If so, then I could transport One Love healing vibrational frequencies to the physical realm of earth and provide healing energies to others.

I looked online for a white crystallized stone, and only came up with white quartz, but that did not really resonate with me.

I stood in the white crystalline space and kept looking inward, in search of something that would help me understand what I was seeing. I was able to see through layer after layer of white crystals.

Finally, I was able to see something that might lead me somewhere! The deeper inward I looked, the white crystals started to give way to white crystals with a yellow-orange tinge. Intuitively, I understood that the healing provided by the yellow-orange-tinged crystalline material would be different than that of the pure white crystals.

I began referring to the healing mountain as "Mount Chakra." The name was created because I needed to have language describing what I had been visualizing.

I was very inspired by learning all of this information. Learning prompted questions on my part. I had an unquenchable desire to know everything *now*. The problem with having questions was that there was not one person who could answer my questions. The only answers could come from my doing further "research" via meditation.

- As I get further in, will the tinge of color become stronger, and provide a more intense level of healing?
- Does the yellow-orange crystal correspond to the second and third chakras and can it provide healing to those chakras?
- Can I do distant healing with the white/yellow/orange crystals or does the person need to be at Mount Chakra energetically in his or her own meditation? (And how would I ever be able to instruct others on how to find what I had been shown?)
- Can I "bring back down" some of this healing power and all-encompassing love to use on others?
- If yes, exactly HOW can I retain the energy, and then direct its use for healing others?

Thinking that crystals really might be an effective medium for transporting Mount Chakra energy, I spent some time searching for a crystal white stone with a yellowish-orange tinge, again to no avail. Most of them were muddy yellow, or dark blotchy orange brown.

Yuck. They were nothing at all close to the vibrant, clean colors that I had seen.

During meditation, I was told that the healing energy I was experiencing was qi (pronounced "chi"), the energy life force that is found in everyone, but a larger amount, and highly concentrated.

CHAKRA HEALING

After my Reiki 2 attunement, I was once again escorted to the healing mountain. This time I was shown that different sections of Mount Chakra contained energies and healing frequencies or vibrations of each of the seven separate chakras. I saw a huge section of red crystalline material for healing of the root chakra, an orange crystalline mass for the sacral chakra, yellow, green, blue, indigo, and violet for the corresponding chakras.

Under my prior hypothesis, I assumed that the direct contact of my skin to the Mount Chakra crystalline structure would be too intense and would feel like I was getting burned. I was surprised that I could touch and actually lie down in each one of the colored crystal areas for a healing, without feeling uncomfortable or like I was getting burned. Furthermore, I received a healing and confirmation of each of the symbols associated with using Reiki on each of my chakras.

I had additional questions:
- If qi is life force and the life force is able to heal, then is that part of God?
- If qi is indeed a part of God, and God is already in

me, then am I part of God? I know some folks who believe that we are all connected energetically, and therefore we are God. I still struggle with my being God.

I was reminded that One Love is of God. I am to teach and heal using One Love. This mountain, Mount Chakra, with healing crystals, is part of One Love. It may be used to help heal chakras in myself and in others.

Alone in a Crowd

I never felt so alone in my entire life. How could I have so many friends, family members, and acquaintances and have absolutely no one that I could talk to about all I was learning? I had shared some of my research with friends, and I heard their polite responses while their eyes glazed over. I didn't want to risk losing friendships or alienating loved ones, so I simply stopped sharing.

Sure, I knew folks that spoke to deceased people and folks that could heal others energetically. But my experiences with vibrational frequencies and One Love were on a whole new level. I scoured the Internet. If I found a snippet that related to my experiences I searched out the authors and learned as much as I possibly could to understand their journey. A lot of times my searches led nowhere.

Sometimes I wondered about my own mental health. How could I be the person that was having these experiences? Was I making all this up in my head? I was always the extremely levelheaded one. How did I get here? I was receiving information that I didn't know existed in the universe, so how could I be making it up?

I believed that there must be other people who were receiving these same energetic downloads that I was. I could not be the only person in the world who was being entrusted with this information.

I continued to take classes and I would talk with my teachers afterwards, trying to make sense of the things I had seen. While they were supportive, none of them had experienced the type of energetic or spiritual journey I seemed to be on. I very badly wanted a mentor, someone who had already been where I was and had come through the other side. But I could find no one.

While searching the Internet, I found Beth Wright from Santa Fe who teaches how to heal chakras. I sought her out, thinking that I might like to learn more about chakra healing. An hour-long appointment with her changed my life. Beth read my energy, provided chakra healing, and confirmed that everything I had been experiencing was indeed real. She explained that I was on a spiritual energetic pathway to becoming a light worker. Light workers are engaged to help promote energetic healing on earth at times when humans need it the most. Like right now.

I am thankful Beth entered my world when she did. Had it not been for her, I probably would have given up. The cognitive dissonance between my physical world and this spiritual realm was creating a chasm between my own inner peace and mental health. I needed to regroup and assimilate the information that I had been given. Beth enabled me to do just that. She helped me know that I was mentally stable and that I was surrounded by spirit guides who were on this amazing spiritual journey with me.

Beth confirmed that indeed, I was to become a teacher and share this journey with others. Whether they believed in it or not was not the question. It was, frankly, not my concern. I was told to put it all in writing, and the people who needed to see it the most would see it.

I still had no one that really understood my journey, but at least I had a few people that validated me in the process. It was up to me to connect with spirit guides that would lead me forward, or I needed to become the mentor that I myself needed. I still felt alone, but at least I didn't feel mentally unstable and alone.

Answers

One particularly trying day, I rallied my guides and started peppering them with questions. Why am I having these experiences? Am I studying the right things? Why am I being told to write it all out?

I received my answers. Loud and clear:
- Shamanism is not the answer.
- Clairvoyance is not the answer.
- God is the answer.

- Love is the answer.
- The golden healing light of God is the answer.
- Spreading the knowledge of God's love is much bigger than a blog or a website.
- It doesn't matter how the word gets out. The word just needs to get out.

CHAPTER
9

Open Clinic

"You are surrounded by animals waiting for healing… Do you want that?" My clairvoyance teacher, Stacia, was giving me an energy reading, and was curious about what she was seeing.

"Yes, I do want that! And I am glad that you see it as well. That absolutely validates what I have been seeing and experiencing!"

I then shared with her my story about Open Clinic and how it came to be.

In February, while meditating, I was being shown a place, a place in an alternate realm, where healing was going to take place. I saw an open-air location with no walls or ceilings. There was a definite front, but not a back. There was space for hundreds or thousands of souls. I was not sure what I was seeing or why I was seeing it. Each day, I meditated and was shown a little more, whetting my appetite to know where all of this was heading. I had been extremely interested in learning about energetic healing techniques, so I was passionately excited about the concept of having a location where I could be of service to healing others, especially spirit to spirit.

I was told the name "Open Clinic." I was shown this name several days in a row, in case I wasn't paying attention. I have learned that Spirit can be quite persistent, repetitive, humorous, symbolic... whatever it takes to get me to pay attention and understand things correctly.

Where is Open Clinic?

Wherever I am standing on a physical plane, Open Clinic is in a different dimension energetically to my right and up three feet or so. I don't know why, but that has consistently been the case.

Animal Spirit Guides: The First Visitors

I have learned that spirit guides can show up in many forms; one just needs to be open to the concept. Animals in meditation or dreams can serve as spirit guides delivering a message.

My first guest in Open Clinic was a turkey. Hmm. What do I do with this? Was this really a turkey that needed healing or was this a message from a spirit guide? I chose the latter. I looked up turkey animal spirit guides on whats-your-sign.com and read that turkeys are the symbol for endings, preparation, and new beginnings. It said: "When the turkey visits us, it is a sign that we must be mindful of the blessings bestowed upon us each day. Further, it is a message to express our strength and brilliance—it's time to show our plumage and reveal our true selves." Gulp. It seemed that I would be going public with all that I had learned regarding intuition and energy. And I could see that this Open Clinic, whatever it was, was truly the beginning of something, and I needed to be present and prepared in order to be part of it.

The next day a camel appeared in Open Clinic. Awesome! I looked up camel spirit animals on sunsigns.org. It read: "The camel animal totem can spiritually provide us with protection and the energy required for endurance. Camels live a life of adversity, residing in harsh climates and environments and enduring long periods of difficulty and strain. Because of the strength of mind that they exert, they serve as a wonderful symbol of a creature's ability to remain positive even during the rockiest of times. They inspire a 'glass is half full' approach to life that we can call upon both daily and in times of seemingly unbearable struggle. The appearance of a camel symbol, in life and in our dreams, can signify difficult times ahead, but the alacrity that they inspire assures us that everything will work out in the end. With their guidance, we can accomplish the impossible, whatever that may be." I could see that Open Clinic would indeed be a journey and process.

Day after day, information about Open Clinic was doled out in small bits. It was maddening at times that I was not given all the information at once, but it gave me time to think things over and try to assimilate the information with what I already understood.

OPEN FOR BUSINESS

I clearly heard the phrase "open for business" and "the Doctor is in," which I found amusing. One, because I do hold a doctoral degree in education, but have purposely chosen to not go by the title of Doctor, and two, because I was reminded of Charlie Brown and Lucy, and how she would hang her "The Doctor Is In" sign up and charge five cents for advice.

I received the message "The Clinic is Open." I understood that it was REALLY open—24/7. My teacher, Stacia, suggested that I hold office hours, and post an energetic sign that I will be at the clinic certain days and times. I was uncomfortable with that concept. I figured if a soul could find its way to the Clinic, then the Clinic would be open.

Next, I had a bear waiting for me in Open Clinic. Back to the Internet and Spiritanimal.info to look up bear spirit animals:

"The bear has several meanings that will inspire those who have this animal as totem:

- The primary meaning of the bear spirit animal is strength and confidence
- Standing against adversity; taking action and leadership
- The spirit of the bear indicates it's time for healing or using healing abilities to help self or others
- The bear medicine emphasizes the importance of solitude, quiet time, rest
- The spirit of the bear provides strong grounding forces

"The bear is also a guide to take leadership in your life or in other people's lives. This animal is feared and admired for its strength. Its presence inspires respect. Its strength and powerful stature will inspire you to step into a leadership role in your life and take action without fear.

"Since the bear is often associated with shamans in many traditions, this spirit animal can symbolize healing abilities and stepping into the role of the healer. If the bear shows up in your life, it may also be time to take care of your own needs for healing, whether it's at the physical, emotional or spiritual level."

I immediately appreciated the message from the bear regarding stepping up into my role as healer. The bear has since made many repeat visits into my meditations and dreams.

THE WISE COUNCIL OF FOUR

In meditation, I was escorted by one of my spirit guides, Reiki, and was shown the waterways on the earth. I saw that Reiki was able to give a healing to the animals and fish that inhabit the earth! How wonderful! I saw that Open Clinic could help animals. Great!

I learned that healing could take place on a physical, mental, or emotional basis. I was also told that the Clinic has always been open, but people just don't know about it. I checked all over the Internet, and did not see any evidence of anyone else writing about a spiritual/energetic Open Clinic concept. If it was always open, does that mean on some spiritual/energetic basis I was always part of it? Or am I just now being introduced to it because I am an interested and willing participant?

In Open Clinic, I had seen my spirit guides, including the Divine Mother, Reiki, Christ-Force, and Man of God there, and I understood that healing could take place any hour, as they were always in attendance when a soul showed up.

I began to call my spirit guides the Wise Council of Four. As I was driving one day, I happened to look up into the sky and saw jet contrails in the shape of the number four. Thank you for the divine reminder that what I am experiencing is real!

OPEN CLINIC EXPANDS

One day, I entered Open Clinic and for the first time I saw souls that did not belong to any animals, but had at one time been in human bodies. How did I know? With the animals, I immediately saw the physical shape of the animal, and I assumed that they had all been in bodies, but had passed on. But here I was seeing grayish cloudy shapes, and when I approached them I could see them in human form and sense or feel what their story was. Over several days during meditation, I witnessed spirits of souls that had passed away from HIV and cancer. I witnessed my spirit guides go to them, provide healing and blessings, and then the souls would move on.

ORDAINED INTO THE MINISTRY

March, 2016. I graduated from my year-long clairvoyance class and received the title of Reverend of the Church of Inner Light. Trying to describe this to my friends and family, I would smile, smirk, and laugh with discomfort. I was sad, confused, and completely bewildered. Shouldn't I be happy having earned this accomplishment?

Feeling particularly unworthy and struggling with what the title of Reverend meant for me, I meditated and asked specifically for guidance and clarification regarding my soul purpose, my new title, and Open Clinic. At the same time, I was listening to one of Stacia's lectures about accepting new healing masters and psychic surgeons as spirit guides. We were encouraged to switch out our healing masters and psychic surgeons if they were ready to transition on, or if I was ready to have a change. Both Peas and Caw said that they were ready to move on. I was very sad to see them go and hoped I had not done anything to turn them away.

As I considered getting a new healing master and psychic surgeon, I specifically stated that I needed "legitimate-looking" guides. First, I requested a new Healing Master. I was amused when I saw an older male with white hair, wearing a white doctor's lab coat. Talk about looking legitimate! I asked him what he wanted to be called, and I heard, "Doc!" Then a psychic surgeon appeared: a younger male wearing blue surgical scrubs, who had a great sense of humor and wanted to be called "Skip." These guides were great!

Then I heard Skip say, "You wanted us to look legitimate so you and others would take us seriously, so now **you** need to be someone that we can take seriously as well!" I knew he was referring to my shrugging off the title of Reverend and being very hesitant to embrace the responsibility of the role. Just then, I felt a large group of souls enter the room and stand to my right. I responded, "Hang on, we aren't ready yet." I don't know how I knew, but I just knew that they were there for healing.

In spirit, Skip came to me and put a minister's black robe on me. I was honored, humbled, and amazed. Then he approached me with a crown of shining stars and went to put it on my head. I was immediately uncomfortable with the thought of being exalted and said, "No! I can't do that!" All of my religious upbringing had focused on worshipping only God, never a person. I would not wear a crown that could make it look like I was trying to be Christ-like. He responded with, "This isn't about *you*! This is about God, and how He will heal *through* you!" Embarrassed, I understood. My role in Open Clinic as a healer was to have God's grace and healing come through me to the souls; I would be nothing more than a conduit. I could do that!

After I had donned the robe and the star crown, I stood in the middle of my spirit guides (the original Wise Council of Four, Doc, and Skip). Together we faced forward, and I saw the throng of souls that had been waiting for us. The first wave felt like hundreds, the second wave thousands, and lastly a hundred thousand! I saw each of the spirit guides circulating, healing, and blessing souls. I stayed front and center, my arms out wide, channeling God's brilliant light, grace, and love to the masses. I felt an amazing connection to an all-loving, non-denominational God of Gods, Lord of Lords. I saw that the other souls understood and accepted their healing and blessings as well. As souls received the healing they desired, they left Open Clinic.

I was able to intuitively understand what some of the stories were. I saw a man who had died of AIDS and needed healing from the traumas of his illness. A child's soul was frightened and received security and comfort when it was connected with a female. Souls that had been disconnected from God, for one reason or another, had been reunited with their Divinity.

What an amazing experience! Afterwards, I realized that I was not physically tired, but exhilarated! Earlier, I had asked for clarification regarding my soul's purpose and the title of Reverend, and now I understood! I had been given a ministry! It was a ministry of attending Open Clinic, and then sharing that news with others, in person and in spirit. I own this ministry and can now accept the title of Reverend with purpose and honor.

In Spirit or in Body?

The second day, I entered Open Clinic and saw a spirit I immediately recognized as my dear friend, Denice! In spirit, I saw a grayish cloud, but intuitively I knew and saw that it was her spirit. I got a little worried, because first, I had only seen animals and deceased persons in Open Clinic, and second, she is very much alive and we would like to keep it that way! I asked her why she was there, and she said that she was curious as to what was going on. When she saw my spirit guides and understood that she could receive a healing, she readily accepted. After she received a blessing from the Divine Mother, Denice flew off as a white dove.

Do all souls with a body fly off as white doves and all those that have already transitioned simply move on when they are done with the healing? Yes. I now understood that Open Clinic could serve both animals and humans, living and deceased, and better yet, I could discern all of those differences. Later, I asked Denice in person if she had been aware of receiving a spiritual healing in Open Clinic, and she said no. That did not deter me from believing in all that I had been shown.

A day later, my sister-in-law Sharon appeared in spirit, received a blessing and also flew off in the shape of a dove. She and Denice are two of my biggest supporters, so it was no surprise to me that they showed up out of curiosity and accepted healing.

Family First

The third morning in Open Clinic, my mother and father, who are still living, were there in spirit. I have not discussed Open Clinic with them in person, but somehow their spirits knew and were curious enough to attend. They were accompanied by a gentleman (also still living) who has a problem with alcohol and drug addiction. I intuitively believed that the gentleman is someone I have known for many years. They all received healing from Divine Mother, Doc, and Skip, and I expected them to leave as soon as they were finished. But they didn't; they just stayed. I told them that they could go, but they said they didn't want to leave.

They said that they wanted to hear the voice of God before they left! Knowing their religious backgrounds, I completely understood their request, although I was surprised by their forwardness. I am not sure that I would be that assertive in person, however, maybe in spirit I am. I wasn't sure what the answer to their request would be. I had already experienced God's healing light shining out through my hands during Open Clinic proceedings and I was secretly hoping that God would speak through me, because I really wanted to experience that also. Instead, God sent a beautiful persimmon-colored energetic healing. What an awesome gift! The colored energy was large enough to surround the three spirits and it radiated soothing unconditional love. I wondered if the orange healing color sent healing specifically to their second chakras, or if it was a more generalized healing. After a few minutes, Mom, Dad, and the gentleman had felt God's presence and were OK to go back to their bodies.

WHO ATTENDS OPEN CLINIC?

Why did some souls desire healing while others were tucked away happily somewhere? I was shown that the bulk of souls not currently in bodies are residing in the Cathedral of Souls. I was not sure what this newfound understanding meant to my pre-existing conceptions of Heaven and Hell, but that didn't seem to be a factor here. I saw that some souls had transitioned out of the physical body, but had not fully passed on, for one reason or another. I believe that the souls in Open Clinic are in the group that needs assistance in order to pass on. They are seeking a healing to complete something that went unfinished here on earth, enabling them to finally complete their journey.

HOW DO SOULS KNOW ABOUT OPEN CLINIC?

I don't understand the communication network that notifies souls about Open Clinic. I think spirits somehow notify other spirits that there is healing available and they just come. I have stopped trying to make it make sense; rather I just accept it as fact and marvel at who shows up.

WHO'S WHO IN OPEN CLINIC?

There were only six healing guides present when I first attended Open Clinic. The line-up of healers changed very quickly soon after, including the addition of three archangels and a few other beautiful healing guides. I have come to truly love each of my guides.

When I enter Open Clinic, I don my minister's robe and then say my hellos to my spirit guides, starting with Divine Mother. She is always behind me over my left shoulder. If you have felt the love of Divine Mother once, you will want to feel it over and over again.

Reiki is always to Divine Mother's right. He presents as a masculine presence and always attends Open Clinic. Reiki uses the ancient energy of Reiki to provide healing.

Next to Reiki, on his right, is a non-denominational healer, Man of God. I am not sure exactly how Man of God assists in healing, but I do know that he is at every Open Clinic. I believe that his presence helps ensure that the healing sessions are respectful, love-filled, and only of high-level vibrational frequencies. The guides and I refer to Open Clinic as "church" sometimes because of the divine nature of healing that takes place there. Man of God is instrumental in "holding space" and preserving the atmosphere of divine healing at Open Clinic.

Christ-Force stands to the right of Man of God during Open Clinic and heals using divine Christ-Force energy, a clear white energetic light. After receiving Christ-Force energy, the recipient feels pure acceptance, compassion, and love.

To the right of Christ-Force and directly behind me is Archangel Raphael, a supreme healer. Archangel Raphael is also called upon to help people while they are traveling. I have seen him heal souls in Open Clinic and felt privileged to have him teach me some lessons about life and healing.

To his right is Archangel Gabriel, a female muse for creativity and writing who is associated with the scribe archetype, as described by Carolyn Myss, in her book *Archetypes: Who Are You?* Every time I stop to say hello to Archangel Gabriel, I know I need to devote some time because, as a muse, she inevitably makes me think about the myriad of things I could be writing about, creating, or studying. She motivates me in amazing ways. I completely lose track of time with her. Some days I know I need to say hello and move on quickly, as I just don't have the time to devote to writing or to one of her other creative ideas. I would need a few more hours in the day to do everything she is showing me.

To the right of Archangel Gabriel is Archangel Michael, the first angel I was introduced to. He is a very large, strong, masculine presence. A supreme healer, he also helps souls transition after death. Every time I have called upon him, I have felt his wisdom, compassion, healing, and protection.

To the right of Archangel Michael and behind my right shoulder is the healing master, Doc, who heals emotions and the chakras. He stands next to the psychic surgeon, Skip, who heals the physical body. In May 2016, Doc was ready to transition out, so he was happily replaced with my first healing master, Peas, and my original psychic surgeon, Caw. They stand in the line-up where Doc used to be, next to Skip.

To Skip's right is Rosa, an American Indian spirit guide I have had with me since birth. Rosa is an older woman with grayish-white hair. She is my connection to the lower world, which is not to be confused with Hell, and has shared insights with me about one of my past lives.

And finally, Doris is an older female presence who oversees my Akashic records. The Akashic records, sometimes called "The Book of Life," refer to a central database of all information (every word, thought, or action) that is stored energetically and encoded for every individual who has ever lived upon the earth. I have learned how to call on Doris when I desire to access or change my records. Doris will also assist me with healing, when someone else's Akashic record keeper needs to know how to change their records.

Each of the spirit guides seems to have their assigned places, and so far, that has never varied.

My familiarity with each of the spirit guides differs. I can always expect a warm embrace from Divine Mother, Reiki, Archangels Raphael, Gabriel and Michael, Skip, Peas, Caw, Rosa, and Doris. The others remain a little more detached and give me a more formal greeting.

THE ROBE

I love my black ministerial robe! I put it on energetically every time that I enter Open Clinic. Different experiences in Open Clinic or in meditation have resulted in changes to my minister's robe, generally in the form of the addition of decorations. It feels like there is some kind of reward system for me, similar to a scout receiving a patch on her vest for learning a new skill. The rewards seem to come when I have been particularly stretched as a student or healer; I never expect these rewards, but am always delighted to see an acknowledgment of my growth! I have not been able to see who puts the new decoration on my robe, but each time I see that something has been changed or added, I have been able to tell why I have received it.

The first reward I was presented was strips of colored glasslike material in differing lengths, approximately one inch wide and two to six inches long, in the colors associated with the chakras (violet, indigo, blue, green, yellow, orange, and red). The strips were arranged in straight lines going down the front of the robe. I first received just a few, but quickly gained more with additional experiences.

CHAPTER 10

Stories from Open Clinic

I have had the profound privilege of witnessing and participating in spirit-to-spirit healing at Open Clinic. While these narratives may seem short, there was a great deal of intensity behind the emotions and healing.

LOVE IS LOVE... IN LIFE OR DEATH

Two of my living friends showed up in Open Clinic one morning. Phil was curious and left after receiving a healing on his knees. Cassandra came and met up with her mother, who passed away several years ago. As they both live in Los Angeles, it was nice to feel like I got to spend time with them in person. I have not told either of them about Open Clinic.

Later that same day, looking out over Open Clinic, I saw a sixteen-year-old who had just died in the hospital after a car accident. She had been escorted to Open Clinic by a handful of her still-living girlfriends; her spirit was a grayish mass and was completely surrounded by their white dove spirits. It was clear that these loving souls had been surrounding her at the moment of death and had such a bond that they wanted to help her transition safely and were protecting her, even in death. Archangel Michael met them, received her, and helped her to move on. Grieving, yet satisfied, the girlfriends flew as doves back to earth. Observing the love between these friends brought tears to my eyes. This was a new one for me. I was accustomed to the idea of loved ones who had already passed on meeting at a deathbed to accompany a soul, but I had never thought about souls with bodies assisting a loved one to pass on.

Fortune Cookies

One evening, I enjoyed a meal of Chinese food with my family. Carefully picking out my fortune cookie, I opened it and read, "Joy will return with the return of a good friend." Cool! I was having fun thinking which friends I hadn't seen in a while.

The next morning, I was beyond delighted to see that my dearest friends, Sylvia and her husband Cliff, both showed up in Open Clinic! Cliff passed away in 2009 and Sylvia in 2013 and I have missed them terribly.

I went to them and embraced them while crying, both in spirit and in person. Divine Mother came to us and I introduced them. She gave both Sylvia and Cliff a hug, and I thought it was because she could see what they mean to me, but maybe it was because of what they mean to her? She gave Sylvia a healing on the trauma from her terminal cancer and gave Cliff a healing from his heart failure and traumatic death. Sylvia put a round, red, glasslike bead on the lapel of my minister's robe. What a blessed treasure!

Then Divine Mother escorted them personally away. I was very sad to see them go, but also delighted for the time that we had been together again. I knew in my heart of hearts that they had not been lingering aimlessly, but had been securely in the Cathedral of Souls.

I asked Divine Mother to take me to the place she had taken Sylvia and Cliff. She took me to the gates of the Cathedral of Souls and we entered together. I felt a little trepidation that a soul with a physical body would not be allowed in, but that was not the case. I guess if Divine Mother takes you inside, who is going to stop her? Inside, I saw Sylvia and Cliff. They were with others whom I have loved and lost in the physical realm: my grandparents on both sides of my family, my cousin Joey, and my friend Parker. I truly reconnected with my friends and family and it brought me great joy, just as my fortune cookie predicted.

I looked down at my minister's robe and saw that one row of round, chakra-colored, glasslike beads had been added around the hem of the robe. As much as I wanted to stay, Divine Mother told me to go spend time in my body with my family and friends on Earth. She then escorted me back to Open Clinic.

Occupational Hazard

Another time, I was drawn to the left side of Open Clinic where I saw a plate of spaghetti and meatballs. I had never seen an object in Open Clinic before, so I was both curious and amused. I could smell the food as I approached. I then saw the spirit of an Italian chef who had passed away. He showed me the kitchen in his restaurant and tables of mouthwatering Italian specialties. The smell of delicious, savory food was overpowering; it was obvious that this gentleman had been incredibly passionate about his craft and had an amazing gift that he freely shared with others. He experienced his spiritual life through the process of creating foods that would leave others tasting God in his food.

I saw that his entire life had been devoted to cooking these foods to share with others, but he had not created a home life or family for himself. While his customers loved his food, few people got to know him closely. He showed me that he died in a fiery explosion at his Italian restaurant. He came to Open Clinic for healing, a closer connection to God, and assistance in passing on.

Anaphylaxis

In Open Clinic, I saw a young father who was in a living body, there with his four-year-old son who was suffering from an anaphylactic allergic reaction. The father was giving CPR to his son. I could feel the father's panic as his son's spirit was slipping away. As the son's body stopped responding to the CPR, it became clear that the father was the one who needed to be healed. Archangels Michael, Gabriel, and Raphael surrounded the two as the drama unfolded. After a few minutes, I watched as the archangels flew off with the spirit of the toddler while the father flew off in the form of a dove, back to his body on earth.

Physician Heal Thyself

I had a fight with my oldest daughter one night. We are very close, so my hurtful words felt really awful to both of us. Apparently, being enlightened in some areas does not make me enlightened in all areas or immune to being a crappy mother on occasion. While we made up that same night, I carried the grief with me into the next morning. With a heavy heart, I slunk into Open Clinic and saw my guides. Knowing they had seen it all unfold last night, there was not much to say, but I was embarrassed. My daughter and I were both hurting and I asked for a healing. I sought the healing not to feel better about myself, but to be able to move on with Open Clinic and my day.

My guides immediately responded. I did not feel the typical healing that I had before, but was surprised when I found myself being totally submerged in a warm energetic bath. It felt like a vibrationally-charged liquid, yet it was dry and wet at the same time. I didn't need to breathe even though I was totally enveloped. While I was marveling at the experience, my rational brain kept trying to decipher and understand what was happening around me and to me. Really feeling the particles swirling around me, I realized that the dry liquid was vibrant with the essence of me-ness. I was completely submerged, yet completely comfortable, for there was nothing present that was not already part of me. I questioned, was I in the amniotic fluid that protected me while in utero? No, there was no essence of my mother's energy, just mine. Only mine. All mine.

I realized that this "essence of me" consisted of more than just the me-ness of my past fifty-five years on Earth. It encompassed the wholeness of me as I was designed from the beginning of my soul's creation. Not just the "me" that is in this lifetime, but the inner essence of what my soul was created from, that has carried from lifetime to lifetime. I immediately thought of the Akashic Records and the storage of all things pertaining to my soul over many incarnations. This bath, this Akashic bath, was profoundly calming and healing. If one subscribes to the theory of one soul experiencing lifetime after lifetime, I found myself wondering if I had taken this same Akashic bath before each lifetime to remind me who my soul was created to be.

This experience was so intense; I could only stay in for a few minutes, although I really just wanted to wallow in it for as long as possible. I could feel healing sensations that were physical in nature and not related to the chakra system. I felt my lungs totally expand; I was able to take such big, deep breaths that it was almost uncomfortable. I felt my pelvic and chest cavities get warm and feel expansive. Being surrounded by me-ness, I felt renewed to my core as to who I was within the larger picture of *who I am*.

After my healing, I searched the internet for information on this Akashic bath. An Akashic bath or pool was referenced in the book: *Do It Yourself Akashic Wisdom. Access the Library of Your Soul* by Jacki Smith and Patty Shaw. How I love it when I read of other people experiencing energy and Spirit like I have.

Right after that, I turned my attention to other spiritual visitors in Open Clinic. Apparently, the theme on this day was that *I* needed healing. The only souls there were the people that I have hurt in this lifetime. I recognized each of them in spirit form and I immediately could see how I had hurt them or caused pain, whether intentionally or unintentionally. I could feel the healing for them and ultimately for me. I received the healing of knowing that my slate had been wiped clean of past hurts and transgressions. This Akashic clean-out enabled forward healing and teaching without being trapped in the energies of the past. I am not perfect, but at least I am not encumbered with guilt or pain.

My guides knew that I needed this time in order to continue to move forward. Thank you for this moment of grace.

Man vs. God

I entered Open Clinic one day and was met by thousands of souls. Very few of them were still in bodies. I understood that these souls were from Europe and many had suffered greatly in the Holocaust. They were very angry with God for allowing them to suffer on earth. They had been holding onto this anger, and as a result, felt alienated from God.

The healing guides went to work as I channeled God's love through my hands. I saw that each soul had a blockage in the seventh, or crown chakra, which restricted the flow of divine love from entering. I understood that the blockages were the result of people's unrealistic expectations of God's role and purpose. The unmet expectations led to hurt and anger, and ultimately the feeling of being abandoned; the end result being complete alienation from God or Divinity. I understood that through the horrors of the Holocaust, God stayed steadfast being God; his love never wavered. I saw that the only thing keeping man from God was man himself.

As the healing session continued, I saw the blockages dissolving, allowing God's love to flow freely and healing to occur. As each soul received healing, they were escorted out by a loving guide.

I had existential questions: Who and what is God? What are God's capabilities for answering prayers in times of excruciating distress? Does God perform miracles? If yes, why aren't they performed more often? Why are some prayers answered, but many more are not? I do not profess to know the answers, but I wondered if perhaps I, and others, had misconstrued the role that God plays in our lives.

I questioned why there were not more souls from the Holocaust in Open Clinic. I understood that many of the people who perished were Jewish and died because of their faith. I was told that they already knew God. These souls that attended Open Clinic had been alienated from God's love and were seeking answers and connection.

I Am Not Worthy

Several other times, I saw souls at Open Clinic seeking reconciliation with God. Each time, I saw they had blocked seventh chakras that were keeping them from connecting with their Divinity. I was able to read the energetic stories in the blockages. Many times it was the person's anger at God that kept them separated. Other times it was a pervasive and paralyzing sense of unworthiness that built the blockage: I am not worthy. How could I possibly love myself? No one would ever want to love me. If they knew what I was really like they wouldn't love me either. God would never love someone like me. I don't deserve to breathe, much less live. During the healing, blockages were dissolved; souls were free to love themselves and accept love from others. These souls were able to receive God's love and were reunited with their Divinity. After the healing, these souls, no longer isolated or adrift, were escorted out.

Man's alienation from God... what an immense concept. I received-chakra colored glass tiles on my robe as a result of my willingness to learn.

Love Lost

In Open Clinic, I saw the spirit of a young Asian man whose girlfriend had taken her life. Also Asian, she had struggled with feelings of unworthiness and despair after her parents spent years telling her that she was an abject failure. The situation was inflamed by her parents' disapproval of her boyfriend. Although she was legally an adult and in college, she desperately sought her parents' approval, not only for her sense of self, but for their status in the community and their financial support. There had been a horrendous confrontation with her parents yelling, belittling, and shaming her. They threatened to disown her if she continued the relationship with her boyfriend. Unwilling to leave him but unable to bear any more grief, she ended her pain by slitting her wrists.

Completely despondent, her boyfriend was in Open Clinic in spirit, trying to decide if he should take his life as well. He could not imagine continuing his life without his girlfriend. His grief was overwhelming and his anger was paramount. My spirit guides surrounded him with healing love; he eventually decided to return to his body on earth.

Healing Grace

This summer, a young girl had an accident on a spinning carnival ride. Her hair became entangled in the machinery and she was virtually scalped. Her doctors were not sure if her eyesight could be saved or not. I had read about her in the news, and was surprised to see her show up at Open Clinic. I recognized her instantly. I asked my guides to please give her healing. I saw my guides surround her and watched as energetic healing took place. I clearly heard the words, "Now go and see!" The next time I read about her in the news, her sight was intact and she was healing beautifully. Thank you, Guides, for your consistent love and willingness to share healing with those who seek it.

Global Warming

Another morning at Open Clinic, Archangel Raphael greeted me with a big hug and Archangel Gabriel was ecstatic because I had come so far with my writing. Archangel Michael seemed a little standoffish. He said that even when I was writing I should be coming to church. I understood. Of course, my apologies! I said good morning to Peas, Caw, Skip, and Doris. I looked out in Open Clinic and saw a vast number of dark, squirming things. I couldn't recognize what they were, but I got the distinct impression they were from the sea and they were all struggling. I heard the words "global warming." I went out to them and put my hands out to channel God's healing to them. I saw that all the guides were still standing in their spots and they beckoned me to join them. Then we all held hands and I saw that the healing was much greater when we stood together and combined our efforts. We stood like that for some time. Then, I tried to leave Open Clinic, but Archangel Michael wanted to teach me one more lesson. He showed me the melting polar ice caps so I could witness that global warming was indeed real.

Angels in Uniform

I recently learned about Flights for Fallen Families, an organization created by Hannah Donato in loving memory of her brother Jake Wykstra. Flights for Fallen Families pays for family members of military personnel to travel to witness the arrival of their fallen relative from overseas, or to attend their memorial ceremonies. Additional information about the organization can be found at www.flightsforfallenfamilies.org.

Since being introduced to Flights for Fallen Families, I have had souls attend Open Clinic who were killed while serving in various branches of the armed services. One of these souls asked me to reach out to his family members to let them know that although deceased, he is not far away in spirit. He told me the nickname he used to call his sister, and shared information about his family. I was reticent, as I didn't want to just drop that news on his family. He came back to me the next day and encouraged me, telling me that I was capable of passing on his message and that his family would receive it with open hearts. They did indeed receive his announcement warmly.

I have witnessed the souls of young men from the military in Afghanistan, as well as young men who lost their lives in Vietnam. They came on different days to Open Clinic; one day there were about fifty men in uniform from the Iraq war and the next day there were about fifty from the Vietnam War. In both instances, I saw the uniforms, the terrain, the sights, sounds, and smells. I felt their fear and saw how each of the soldiers present had died. They all received healing from their own personal traumas and received assistance in transitioning over.

There was one visitor that I was willing but unable to assist, at least in person: I was told the name David Frank Martin, and the words "Vietnam War veteran," "Texas," and "Fort Hood." He was young, Caucasian, had dark hair and a black mustache, and told me that he was proud to have served in Vietnam. He shared that he left a baby daughter stateside, named Darla. He wanted me to share with her that he never stopped thinking of her, and living to see her again is what kept him going. Unfortunately, I was unable to find any information that would help me find her, or his identification, through the internet. David, you will need to tell me more if I am to be successful in connecting with Darla in person. I did, however, pass on the information spirit to spirit.

I was new to listening to the spirits of the deceased and trying to reach out to their families in turn. I was rewarded for my risk taking with the gift of more chakra-colored strips on my robe.

Working the Late Shift

In my typical fashion, I woke up, meditated and entered Open Clinic. Wearing my black robe, I turned to greet my guides. But something felt different. I approached Divine Mother and she smiled, but did not embrace me as she normally would. Reiki also smiled, but had no hug for me. I thought it odd, but at the same time, I didn't feel as if I had been away from them, so even I did not feel a hello hug was warranted.

Then I understood. We had learned about astral travel in my coursework. My astral body must have been at Open Clinic while I slept. I wonder how many times that has happened!

I'm Looking for You

After class one day, four of us students decided to go have lunch. We discussed our class and where we were on our personal journeys. I shared Open Clinic with my classmates for the first time. I was a little hesitant, but thought I needed to let them in on my experiences. If I could not share this with the few people in the world that could grasp the concept, I had no business trying to write a book about it.

Delphine said, "Oh! What I saw in class makes sense now!" A senior high student from a neighboring school was co-captain of the cross-country team. During the last track meet, he simply dropped dead. It was tragic for all involved. She said this same young man showed up in class today in spirit asking for help. She did not know how to help him and apologized. After I explained about Open Clinic, Delphine said, "He must have been looking for you."

After lunch, I promised Delphine I would try to get him the healing he needed to transition over. I remembered reading that sometimes when a person dies quickly and unexpectedly, their souls do not transition right away. They may linger in some sort of nowhere until they can get help to pass over. I drove home and went energetically to Open Clinic.

I have always just looked around Open Clinic to see who happened to show up in spirit. I never went with the hopes of seeing anyone in particular. With my minister's robe on, I said, "I want to see the young man who was in class today looking for assistance." I was immediately pulled up and out of Open Clinic. I saw Open Clinic become smaller and smaller until it was a pinpoint below me. I felt like I was floating in dark outer space. I wondered if I was out on the "Threshold," the space where souls linger before birth, after death, and between lifetimes, but it felt much more nebulous than that. I was just floating. Somewhere. Anywhere. Nowhere.

I asked again (into black nothingness) for this young man to join me in Open Clinic. After my request, I was brought back down to Open Clinic as quickly as I went up. Back in Open Clinic, I looked and saw this young man had shown up!

Somehow, I had gone out and requested his spirit to come forward and join me. Did this mean now I could go out and summon spirits of particular individuals? I always wondered how mediums could find souls that people were requesting to speak with. Maybe I had just figured it out!

I saw other souls waiting in Open Clinic, but I concentrated on this young man since he had actively sought assistance earlier. I felt his fear and apprehension, but it dissipated quickly as Divine Mother, Archangel Michael, and Archangel Raphael surrounded him. I saw that as he was receiving healing his energy shifted for his transition. His loved ones still reeling from his loss received a healing as well. When he was finally at peace, I saw Divine Mother escort him out. I then turned my attention to the rest of the souls in Open Clinic.

Ministry Through Intercession

In Open Clinic one day, I heard laughing. It did not sound like regular, happy laughter. No, this was maniacal laughter. These were souls of people who had been deeply compromised, emotionally and mentally; in layman's terms, I would describe them as criminally insane. Why were they here in Open Clinic? I saw that they had murdered others as a result of their mental illness and were estranged from any kind of connection with God.

I immediately jumped down, in spirit, and stood right next to them and tried to channel God's healing energy. I was stepping in dark sludge and getting totally covered in brown energetic gunk. My guides pulled me back up to the dais and cleaned me off. They explained that I would be more effective by holding space and sending healing from afar. They showed me how to help by shifting energy in the minds of these souls to free them from their distorted thinking, which was keeping them from knowing God. This shifting of energy allowed God's energy to have direct access, in order to provide healing.

Isn't God capable of simply providing healing to every soul? I assume so. Why doesn't God just heal every soul without another person intervening or praying for them? I don't know. Why would God wait for a soul to show up at Open Clinic before providing a healing? I don't know. I just know that when these souls showed up at Open Clinic and received a healing, their energy shifted in their crown chakras and the Divine healed them.

After this experience, I understood another facet of my ministry: shifting energy when a person or soul cannot shift energy on their own. This allows for transformation so divine healing can occur.

CHAPTER
11

Life Lessons in Open Clinic

I am certain that I have grown personally, spiritually, and as a healer because of the lessons I have learned from observing what happens in Open Clinic. I have no question that lessons have been provided for my own personal growth as well as spiritual and energetic healing for others.

For example, one day, the soul of a female teen was there for healing. She had died of a drug overdose. I felt myself judging her for the choices she made that brought her to the overdose. As the mother of teenage daughters, my judgment was infused with fear. Archangel Raphael came up behind me and gave me a healing to my heart chakra. I understood that there was no room for judgment in Open Clinic; just compassion. It was not my place to judge, but to assist with healing.

From One Mother to Another

Many years ago, our family travelled to China with some friends. My friend took some photos of street scenes to commemorate our visit. One of the photos was of a young woman with a toddler, sitting in the gutter begging. The photo captured grief and embarrassment in the young mother's eyes and I was embarrassed too, that we had memorialized this low point in her life.

I recognized this same mother in Open Clinic one morning. She was there to explain something to me, more than for her own healing. She wanted me to know that she was killed some time after the photo was taken. She had been called lazy for begging in the street, and was kicked and brutally beaten by a male stranger. She explained to me that she wasn't lazy, that she was despondent and had given up all hope of being able to care for herself or her child. She said that a lot of people that are begging are despondent and have totally given up any hope. She showed up to teach me that judgment has no place in Open Clinic or here on earth. Thank you for the timely lesson!

Oh, Baby

One morning, Open Clinic was full of very small grayish souls. I looked closely and saw that they were aborted fetuses. I went forward to be with them and I asked, "What was that like? Will that experience carry with you as you move forward from life to life?" I very clearly heard the words, "I forgot to know." I took that to mean that these souls would not carry grief or trauma to their next lives as a result of the abortions. Each of them had an angel come hold them lovingly and carry them off.

I asked if we could please give a healing to all of the souls of the babies that had been aborted. They could not all fit into Open Clinic, so they stayed where they had been residing out on the Threshold and received healing. Then thousands of angels came, one for each baby soul, and took them off, heading to the Cathedral of Souls. Will there be an energetic shift in that realm as a result of removing all of these young souls?

One soul stayed as the others were taken out. Why was this soul still here? What was I to see or learn from this little one? Then I saw the faces of this baby's parents. I did not know the mother, but I immediately recognized the father as someone I have known for some time. Years ago, he told me about an unplanned pregnancy that happened while he was in college. The mother had the baby aborted without much discussion; my friend did not have a say in the decision that would affect all of their futures. He described the ensuing grief and imminent breakup of their relationship. I felt the father's genuine sadness over the years, as he wondered about the child he would never know.

And here I was with the beautiful male soul that had been let go all of those years back. I held it. Knowing the loss that the father had suffered, I held it longer and closer. I realized that the loss of this soul from our planet was also my loss, as I might have known him through his father, had he been born. I asked that this little one receive a special healing. As he was receiving the healing, his energy as a soul started to get larger and started to look older. Was this soul ready to be in a body now? I felt the pain of the mother's and father's sadness and grief. Was there just a shift in energy that allowed this baby's soul and the parents to all heal?

Where does my judgment about the circumstances enter in? I realized that it doesn't. A minister at church blesses the souls in front of him, but doesn't curse the person who caused the hurt.

YOUR JAIL OF MY MAKING

At Open Clinic, I was given a wooden dresser drawer to look through. Even more interesting, as I held it, the drawer became life-sized. Not sure what to expect, I started examining the contents. I saw trapped souls. These trapped souls were all living people that I know! What? I didn't understand. Then, I saw that they had all been trapped by *my* own words or perceptions over the years! I was shown that when I spoke of someone in a critical or judgmental way, I condemned the person to be stuck in my perceptions of them, as if they had remained exactly the same, even though time had passed. By repeating their stories or continuing to see them in an unfavorable light, I did not allow them the grace to be in real time, or recognize their freedom to change, grow, and evolve.

And so, I reminded myself to not speak ill of anyone. Their actions were in the past; the person may have changed considerably since that incident, and I need to respect, honor, and encourage that. Every morning, each one of us wakes up with infinite possibilities to re-create who we are and who we want to become. Surely I want others to see me and know me for who I am in real time, and not who I used to be in the past.

A Mother's Love

In Open Clinic, I saw the souls of a young pregnant mother and her unborn baby girl who had both just died in a car accident. They were accompanied in spirit by her two-year-old daughter, who had been severely injured and was lingering between life and death.

I saw her father, in body, crying over his injured daughter in the hospital, begging for her to fight to live and choose life with him. He could not bear to lose his wife and both children at the same time.

The mother's spirit did not want to be separated from the toddler and wanted all three "girls" to be together. I understood that she wanted her two-year-old daughter to transition over and remain in spirit with her. My initial response was, "How could you do that to her father?" I was shown that this was not a selfish request on the mother's part. The mother thought that the toddler would be safer if she were in spirit rather than in a body back on earth.

For the first time, I understood the difference in perspective between "life" to a human in a body and "life" in the spirit realm. While in a body, there is no greater desire, no greater need, than that of staying alive. Hang on… you can't leave me now… just keep breathing… stay with me. However, in the spirit realm, there isn't time or space. No beginning or end. Spirits who have transitioned over are at peace. There is no lack, no desire. Spirits just are. Spirits in the spiritual realm have no burning desire to be anything or anywhere other than what and where they are.

I saw the struggle that the daughter's soul was facing: should she stay in comfort with her mother and sister? Or face life without them and stay in her body on earth with her father? I observed as Divine Mother approached them and gave the mother and baby in utero healing so they could continue transitioning over. She allayed the mother's fears of being separated from her older daughter; they would indeed be reunited again one day. Divine Mother then gave the toddler a healing. Not wanting to abandon her father, I saw that the little girl decided to continue life on earth. Divine Mother then escorted the toddler's soul back to the hospital and her father.

The Clinic is Open 24/7

Another morning in Open Clinic, I zipped up my black robe and walked in. I saw Mi, my higher self, and my healing guides; they had been together providing healings in my absence. Was that even a possibility? Could my higher self be attending church while I was living my life down here on earth? Yes, I believe it can happen, because I saw it.

What a gift! What a relief! I was feeling guilt and self-loathing because I was not spending as much time at Open Clinic as I wanted to or thought I should. I was reminded that there was no room for judgment for others, or even myself, at Open Clinic. Thank you, Mi, for helping me be in two places at once.

CHAPTER 12

The Intrepid Traveler

IN THE ARMS OF THE ANGELS

Archangels Raphael and Michael use Open Clinic as a time to take me places to teach me lessons. They energetically tuck me under their really large wings and literally just start flying, with me in tow. The first time I was a little frightened, but mostly exhilarated! I could feel the air rushing by me and the force or pressure against my body from the fast travel, or from a quick stop. I am not aware of any boundaries beyond which we cannot go, although my guess is archangels might also have their limits.

Some of the more memorable things I have been shown include:

Archangel Raphael flew me over Honduras. I was very afraid. I saw many souls that had transitioned out of their bodies, but hadn't passed over, hanging like a thick fog over the city. I wondered if all those souls meandering about made it harder for souls in bodies to connect with Spirit or God. Archangel Raphael then flew me over the USA and I saw my own parents. I was reminded that there is a great deal of healing that is needed here at home as well.

Archangel Michael took me for a flight. I was nervous and laughing. How rare it is for me to laugh out loud. He took me to a land of angels, all different sizes, but angels nonetheless. He explained that all of the angels had different purposes. Archangel Michael told me to call on angels when I needed assistance.

Then Archangel Michael tucked me under his wings and we took off. How quickly we were in outer space. It was no longer a light blue sky but it was very black with stars. I realized that almost right outside Open Clinic is outer space! Back at church, I looked around and saw that the clinic was filled with non-earthlike creatures, or aliens, curious about Open Clinic. The aliens took on different forms, not gray and shapeless like souls, but had distinct shapes of various shapes and sizes. They did not look like humans. I could not sense a soul-like aliveness or presence, nor did I sense any "niceness" or welcoming approachability. I searched for a sense of morality or amorality and found neither. I could not sense whether or not they had any connection to God or Spirit. I felt a clear shield being placed around me at the same time

I felt energetic resistance behind me. I understood that the others were there to observe and gather information about healers and healing techniques. Looking at my team of healing guides, and thinking that the aliens were probably not at all interested in God-based healers, I thought they might be the most intrigued with Reiki, Doc, and Skip. I heard Archangel Michael say that the angels don't have anything to do with aliens because the aliens never call on the angels. He further explained that humans are different and will readily call on the angels for assistance. My guess is that the aliens left probably rather unimpressed.

A few weeks later, Archangel Michael took me to the outer edges of our universe. Again, I saw a line-up of alien ships sitting along the horizon, as if just watching mankind from afar. After these experiences, the only thing that would surprise me would be if we ever had undeniable proof that there were *no* alien life forms among us.

Archangel Michael took me on a flight that was very far away. For the third time, I saw alien ships on the horizon. I waited to see why I was being shown this. I was told that once mankind destroys itself, these non-human aliens will move in and inhabit the earth.

THE RAINBOW BRIDGE

During our hamster Sundae's misadventure, when he got himself wedged between the drywall and our bathroom cupboard, I was able to use my skills as an animal communicator to connect energetically with Sundae. I could feel his enjoyment of the adventure, which later turned into dehydration and angst as he tried to escape his small, dusty prison. Calling on my spirit guides, Sundae and I were gifted with serenity and calm, and he was protected during our loud, wood-splintering efforts to rescue him.

The next morning I went into Open Clinic. As is my custom, I said hello to each one of my guides starting with the Divine Mother. As I came to Archangel Michael, he took me up in his strong wings and started to fly. I realized that he was taking me back to a time in my childhood when my small, white hamster was dying of wet tail. I saw and remembered the experience vividly. I was about eight years old and was holding my hamster in my hands, trying desperately to heal it. I think I had some memory of being able to heal through my hands in a past life and was trying to re-create that ability. I remembered and saw that I was very upset that I was not able to heal my hamster. I also saw that Rosa, one of my spirit guides, had been there with me all those years ago while I prayed for the ability to heal.

Archangel Michael and I returned to Open Clinic. There were some beings in the clinic and as I went to see them, I realized that they were all the animals that I had ever loved. They were all there in spirit. I realized that I have always had a strong attraction and devotion to animals and continue to surround myself with them.

I saw our first dog; a black toy poodle named Petite, along with our childhood parakeets, Sagebrush and Tumbleweed, whom I didn't mind feeding, but hated cleaning up after. I saw my cockapoo Bailey, a beautiful soul, who was my heart and soul during my divorce in my late twenties. I saw a line-up of each turtle, hamster, gerbil, chameleon, fish, my kitty KT, and our rabbit, Shivers.

I saw the tadpoles that I had played with as a child in a drainage pond close to my grandparents' home in their fruit orchard. I saw myself on a wooden raft playing in the murky water with my brother, and I saw that my treatment of the tadpoles had been respectful and one of awe for nature.

I saw the minnows that I used to play with in run-off water at the end of our street, long before they put in an overpass and main thoroughfare. Again, I saw that my interactions with the fish and snails had been respectful.

Then I saw the daddy-longlegs. Gulp. We used to have a sandbox in our backyard and I would spend hours playing in the sand making mud and enjoying anything that crawled near me, the victims usually being daddy long-legs and roly polys. I saw myself as a child playing with the daddy long-legs and pulling off their legs. I felt an audible gasp, pain, and suffering. I was immediately filled with grief and regret for having been callous to a living being as a child. I was told that I didn't know any better at the time.

Archangel Michael then took me to another realm, which was further out to my right and higher in elevation. This place was filled with animal spirits. I saw all kinds of animal spirits together. I did not see a separated area for each of the different animal types. On the outskirts of this animal realm I saw a rainbow. I chuckled.

I had always found the concept of "The Rainbow Bridge" to be somewhat trite. I could not imagine passing away and then seeing a rainbow that I would cross over and find the spirits of my beloved animals that had passed over before me. I thought this notion found in condolence cards and children's books was simply created to help grieving pet owners feel better about being reunited someday.

Having not ever believed in the concept of a rainbow bridge, I felt silly for asking, but I did anyway. "Is that really the Rainbow Bridge?" I was told, "So many people think there is one, so there can be one if people want it to be real." Fascinating, Archangel Michael, thank you for showing me all of this.

SANTA FE

Last spring my family and I traveled to Santa Fe and stayed near the plaza. Every time I had gone to Santa Fe, I felt a strong energetic connection, but what I was connecting to was never clear. I felt this same energy during this trip, but this time, I was able to better understand the energetic pull this region had on me.

Santa Fe: Lower World

During meditation, I was shown a new (to me) realm that is to the right of Open Clinic and down about six feet, which is still about three feet higher than our earthly reality. I was in an ancient setting. The soil was a dry, dusty red and there were hundreds of American Indian souls. Men, women, and children, they were all very angry at God for the genocide against them (I am starting to see a pattern here: people feeling alienated from God because of their unfulfilled expectations). I asked my healing guides to join me to provide healing for those souls that were interested. Divine Mother played a huge part in providing the healing. My guess is that Divine Mother was already a familiar, loving entity of theirs.

I realized that maybe Open Clinic can take place anywhere spirits and my healing guides are willing to meet.
    After that healing, one of the glasslike strips was taken off my minister's robe and was replaced with a strip of the same size that was some sort of metal in a rose-gold color. Soon thereafter, I learned about Shamanism's Upper, Middle, and Lower World. I believe I had witnessed Lower World, which is not to be mistaken for Hell.

Santa Fe: Rosa

On our first night in Santa Fe, I had a very vivid dream that I was given the gift of a scorpion from an older female American Indian spirit guide, whom I had seen at

Lower World. When I awoke, I looked up the symbolism behind the scorpion. It symbolized transformation, rebirth, protection, and isolation. I very much appreciated the gift and felt the spiritual protection that the scorpion represented. It was a good reminder to me to keep my own spiritual guard up while working with other spirits.

In meditation, I returned to the Lower World. I saw that I was wearing all black, presumably because my minister's robe was too formal. I saw the same spirit guide as in my dream; she was wearing two scorpions on her right wrist and had a scorpion tattoo over her right shoulder. I clearly saw that she used the scorpions for protection; no one would dare mess with her. I thanked her for the scorpion protection. I asked what she wanted to be called and heard, "Rosa." I was told that she had been with me since birth. Indeed, I could see that my Higher Self had known Rosa all along and had gone with her to this Lower World many times. I saw my Higher Self dancing happily with the others. Rosa showed me around the Lower World. There were many American Indians there, not seeking healing, but simply residing there in spirit. In hindsight, I appreciate that my conscious mind was being made aware of my history in the spiritual realm.

During our second night, I was woken from a deep sleep because Rosa wanted to make me aware of something. She escorted me back to the Lower World. All of the American Indians were in one area. Groups of others were somewhat segregated by race in other areas further off. Rosa then replaced two glass strips on my minister's robe with rose-gold metallic strips. She placed them low, by my left knee. I asked her why they were placed there. She said they were placed low to remind me about humility—they were not placed up high because that would come across as showy.

Still sleepy, I entered Open Clinic. Rosa had ceremoniously joined the lineup of healers in Open Clinic, and I was happy to welcome her. I saw four American Indians on horseback facing away from me. All four were decorated with feathers and leather and seemed to hold much power and respect in their group. The third from the right seemed to be the leader, being more decorated than the others. I was too tired to hold a service and fell back asleep.

Early the next morning, I woke and headed back into Open Clinic. The three horsemen and the chief were still on their horses, facing away from me. I looked past them and finally understood what was going on. In front of them were thousands of American Indians waiting for healing! The healing by my guides and God through me was short. When it was complete, they all flew off like doves. They were all still alive in bodies! My guides and I smiled and laughed at the sight. The chief looked over his left shoulder at us and said something that felt like a thank you. Then the four on horses disappeared. Several more of my glass strips were replaced with rose-gold strips. Beautiful! And thank you!

Santa Fe: Understanding the Pull

My third night in Santa Fe, Rosa took me again to the Lower World. She showed me the following scene: A young American Indian woman in her late twenties with long brown hair whose name was Sana. I felt that my soul was connected to her. Was this woman named Sana me in a past life? Could this be why I have a pull toward Santa Fe, its red soil, foods, and strong females in the Indian culture?

Sana had three children: a young son age seven, a two-year-old daughter, and a female baby. Her strong young husband came in, drunk, and started fighting with her because she had given him another daughter, which he felt as a huge disappointment. He continued to argue while she tried to quiet him so he wouldn't frighten the children. He pushed her and she fell and hit her head against the stone floor. She died as a result of the head injury.

I looked around the room and saw who was going to ultimately raise Sana's (my) children: an older Auntie and Uncle. I immediately recognized them as my much-loved friends from my current life, Sylvia and her husband Cliff! The Auntie was ever so loving and doting, while the Uncle was gruff towards Auntie and the children, but deep down I could see he loved them all deeply.

At that moment, I had so many questions answered. Ever since I met Sylvia and Cliff, we shared such an intense connection, which made no sense, given the limited time we shared together. Even though Sylvia and Cliff have both passed away, I have been told that Sylvia and I are still connected spiritually by a golden thread. I love it!

Santa Fe: Don Diego and the Priest

At the bed and breakfast, I was very aware of a cat and a Catholic Priest, both residing there in spirit form. While sitting at breakfast, the cat made itself known to me by sitting in the sun on the table behind me. Then it walked between my legs, rubbing itself against me, its tail straight up. I clearly had the impression that it was purring, and very happy to be noticed.

I asked the homeowner, Anne, if a black and white cat had lived there. Anne laughed as she told me the stories of Don Diego, the cat that had arrived one day as a kitten and made the bed and breakfast his own. Don Diego took up residence in the parlor while breakfast was being served and would sit in the sun, as I had experienced. He would sit outside the bedroom doors of the customers that welcomed him and gave him snacks, and he ignored those patrons who were not cat lovers. He would climb the apple tree and not be able to climb back down, and Anne would climb up after him and help him. She shared that the cat was so comfortable at the inn that he would lie in the middle of the busy street sleeping; she had to move him several times in his old age, so he would not get run over. Eventually Don Diego died of old age, and Anne still missed him terribly.

The cat was entertaining to me, while the priest was really not very entertaining at all, because he stuck to me like glue. I was first aware of the priest while I was meditating in our room. I felt a dark uneasiness in his personality, making me think that if he had been my priest, I would have changed churches. I asked him to step out, that we would only be there three nights, and after that he was more than welcome to return. While he did leave our bedroom, I would see him outside in the courtyard, and I even felt his presence near us around town. I could see that the priest had been manipulative, disagreeable, inappropriate with females, had taken his own life, and had been hanging out unhappily ever since.

Back in our hometown, I meditated and immediately saw that the priest had followed me home. Sometimes, I think spirits who have not transitioned over are relieved to see someone who can acknowledge their existence, so they keep hanging around trying to get assistance. I was not pleased to see him. I told him to either go back to Santa Fe, or to come to Open Clinic for assistance, but it was not acceptable to hang around my home. That next morning, he walked in to Open Clinic. Archangel Michael worked with the priest, escorted him out, and helped him transition over. Afterwards I had no more visits from the priest.

Lilac Planet

During meditation, I asked to be taken somewhere so I could see what other healing methods were available. I could not see who was leading me, and I was whisked away to a place that seemed to be outside our atmosphere. Our travel was so fast that I could feel the pressure on my body pushing me out and away from the earth. As we neared our destination, the force pushing on my body changed to a force pulling me toward the new location.

Everything was a lilac color, almost as if I had lilac-colored filters over my eyes. This place was clearly not Earth. There were no buildings, structures, or life forms as I would recognize them. I stood on the lilac land and sensed that it was a healing energy. I could pass through it, yet it wasn't hollow, gel-like, fluid, or transparent. At the same time, I felt it pass through me. I was not afraid, but curious. I felt healing in my chest that was clearly not related to the chakras or to a typical physical healing.

Interestingly, when I came out of meditation, I realized that I had no other memories of this trip to Lilac Planet after the healing, although my clock indicated I meditated for some time. There was something creepy and concerning about having no memories although I know I spent more time there. I was feeling uncomfortable with this, had a nagging ache in the pit of my stomach, but oddly, I was intrigued and wanted to understand more.

Lilac Planet: Round Two

A few weeks later, I returned to the Lilac Planet. The return trip was less pleasant. I was met by a lilac-hued man who looked similar to a human, but I had the clear sense that he was not. I wondered if he was presenting as a human so I would not be frightened. This guide took me to other lilac-hued persons and animals. As I looked at them they started smiling and laughing and then all of their mouths started sagging as if melting. I was frightened for a minute, but I wanted to understand more.

I could not communicate with them and I understood that communicating would require a form of trance-mediumship, where my mind would be entered energetically, so they could speak through me. I was not willing to participate.

In my real body, I felt a searing pain in my left foot, which was relieved when the guide gave me a sip of a white tea-like drink (I am still surprised at myself that I drank it, even on an energetic level). I understood that this drink was giving me the gift of being able to understand and communicate with the members of the Lilac Planet, who communicated only through symbols. I told them quite clearly that they were not to energetically enter my mind. Only I was to be in my body or mind, but that I was willing to communicate on their behalf for them.

Shortly after I sipped the drink, I felt a huge energy shift in my third and second chakras; I felt a strong sense of ability and assuredness. The guide sat me down at a table with an older lilac gentleman whom I was to try to understand. I started receiving images in my mind of symbols, all in black and white, some which were recognizable, most of which were not. I did not see any discernible letters. The symbols came very quickly. After a few minutes, I stopped receiving symbols and we were finished. I wished that I had pen and paper in real life, so I could have jotted down the images I was seeing to review them later.

It was clear that they had no interest in me as anything other than a means to an end. This was a test to see if I was capable of receiving and deciphering the elder's information, and I was. There were no pleasantries;

I felt like they saw me as a commodity that was wholly expendable, and even though they needed me, somewhat reprehensible.

I heard the words "the wisdom of the ages" loudly and clearly. The wisdom of the ages... I took that to mean these beings had been around for many, many years, perhaps a lot longer than humanity, and I could learn from all they had experienced. I also understood that this information from the Lilac Planet would be interesting, perhaps beneficial, to humans and I could be the carrier of that information, if I wanted to become their voice. I had very mixed emotions about the prospect of becoming the voice for non-human beings.

I went to Open Clinic and I was crushed to see that all of my glass chakra-colored strips had fallen off of my minister's robe! The only decorations remaining were the rose-gold metallic strips from Rosa, the round beads around the hem and the red one on my lapel from Sylvia. I wondered if that signified I was done learning about chakra healing and ready to move on to something else. I had a sinking feeling that my healing guides had not appreciated my visit to the Lilac Planet and that I was getting off on a wrong track somewhere. Maybe that was the real reason that many of my medallions had fallen off my robe.

Still, I expected to see a purple circle medal on my robe for my time at the Lilac Planet. I had received decorations on my robe for going through so many of my learning experiences—surely I would receive one for going to the Lilac Planet. Nope. Sigh. For the first time ever, I put a medal on my robe myself, and felt a little sneaky for doing so. It was a purple round medallion. It was appropriately lilac in color, and I was pleased to see that it glowed.

I went to greet the Divine Mother and give her a hug. She hugged me but not as close as usual. She looked at me and said, "You glow of lilac." And I saw that she was right. She said, "You shouldn't glow at church." I removed the glowing lilac medallion and vowed to myself not to reward myself again, that the decorations were gifts from my guides.

I stepped aside and did a white light healing and saw that I had lilac beings inside me. I was not happy that the lilac beings had violated the rules that I had set up just yesterday. I was very clear—do not enter my being without my permission, yet here they were. I vowed to stay clear of the Lilac Planet and all of its inhabitants. I was reminded that alien life forms do not necessarily subscribe to human mores and rules of morality. It was rather pointless to ascribe those qualities to them or assume that they should abide by them. These lilac beings were opportunistic, manipulative, and not to be trusted.

That same morning at Open Clinic, I saw a lilac spokesperson on the outer edge of Open Clinic. I noticed the Divine Mother had an angry, disdainful reaction to his being there, but she did not say anything. I asked him why he was there. He showed me that he just wanted to look around to see what I did there. I felt a little wary, somewhat violated, and yet a little honored that I was being sized up. I told him that he could look and then he needed to leave. I told him that he had violated my rule of entering my personal space and that was not acceptable.

I then heard myself thinking that I needed to practice drawing the Lilac Planet symbols so I could do it well. I must have been somewhat intrigued by the ability to understand and speak for this group, or maybe I was intrigued that they wanted help from *me*. Why wasn't I furious that, once again, I had been manipulated and violated? How is it that these lilac beings had some hold on my thoughts that made me consider helping them?

Lilac Planet: Round Three

What was it that continued to intrigue me about the Lilac Planet? Was it slightly flattering to think that I offered something special that could help a whole other species?

I journeyed up to the Lilac Planet one more time, even though in the back of my mind I was thinking, "No, Ruth, this isn't in your best interest. Just stop." I was quite surprised by my willingness to do something in spirit, that in body I thought was a bad idea! I can see how people get lured into trouble if they don't set clear limits for their involvement in the other-worldly dimensions.

I was met by a lilac-hued guide who introduced himself as Samuel. Feeling emboldened by my anger at feeling violated and manipulated earlier, and thinking that this group needed me more than I needed them, I asked,

"Why is everything lilac?" Samuel said, "Because that is how you wanted it. Because then you weren't afraid."

Great. I was being manipulated again. This group had determined what would bring me into their confidence, and used it to give me a false sense of comfort. I had a sickening feeling.

I said that if I chose to dictate their symbols into English print, I would need some form of transmitter or translator so I could analyze what was being said to me. I was handed an energetic gadget that would be placed inside my head that would enable me to decode their symbols.

I saw a person-like figure sitting at the table; I assumed it was the same elderly figure that had tested me on my previous journey. I had a sense that he was the keeper of the information for this group and that he was the one I would be receiving information from. I wondered if there were only a few individuals left in this lilac population, and if that made finding a human translator even more urgent.

As I approached the elderly man, all of the lilac color faded away. He was no longer lilac in color and neither were the table or surroundings. For the first time, I was seeing things on the Lilac Planet that were typical colors. Part of me was pleased that the facade had come down, but still angry and on alert. I had learned to question everything. How could I have any trust for anything that I was seeing, no matter what color? Was this "man" really a man or some other oddly shaped creature temporarily in the shape of a human so I would not be frightened?

For some inexplicable reason, I continued. "Why should I channel for you?" I heard, "We have been waiting for someone like you to share our information with humans."

I responded with, "What is so special about *you* that I would spend my time and energy and risk my hard-earned reputation on you?" Clearly, everyone I knew would think I was nuts if I channeled information from an alternate realm. There was no answer.

With that, I placed the transmitter on the table and said thanks, but no. I left the Lilac Planet and never returned. These beings had no respect for my boundaries and were simply trying to fulfill their own agenda, whether it was good for me or not. I decided not to think about them or be open to them in any way again.

. . .

In my quest to learn everything there is to know and experience all things energy, had I left myself open and vulnerable to things I had no business being involved in? Had I walked into situations that I wish I hadn't? The Lilac Planet comes to mind. While I learned a great deal from each of the experiences I had, I am still stunned and amazed that I could let myself get connected with something that was clearly not in my best interest. As I tell my daughters, "If you don't stand for something, you will fall for anything." I appreciate my newfound understanding of how someone can get off on the wrong track, and am profoundly grateful that I did not spend any more time and energy on it than I did.

CHAPTER
13

Journey of the Soul

One morning, Archangel Raphael flew me out to what I understood to be "out on the edge before time." As we were soaring together through a black universe, I was shown my life as if it was on a timeline, starting with present time and reversing so I could watch myself getting younger. We continued moving backwards through time, and I was shown recognizable excerpts from my life from when I was a young adult, then teenager, and child. Then I saw myself as a toddler and lastly a baby.

Next, I saw myself inside my mother's uterus, continuing to get smaller and smaller. I heard the beating of my mother's heart and the flushing of fluids around me, observed the utter darkness and felt the warm compactness of being inside her. As the images of "me" in utero continued to get younger and smaller, I witnessed each of the stages of my fetal development, but in reverse. Eventually I was nothing more than four cells, reducing to one, a zygote, the cell created by the coming together of a sperm and egg. I could sense the energy of both my mother and my father in this cellular creation.

Moving further back in time, I experienced the zygote, my zygote, dividing and becoming a separate sperm and egg. I let out an audible gasp as I experienced my sense of wholeness, humanness, being pulled apart chemically, emotionally, and spiritually.

My nothingness was then cast into darkness. I was a speck of orange-yellow floating in darkness... waiting and floating. I was present, observing where my soul, or spirit, was *prior* to the moment of my own conception! I have since learned that this place where souls linger before birth, after death, and between lifetimes is called the "Threshold" or the "I Am."

I had been floating peacefully, calmly, in what appeared to be a black, quiet void of nothingness, when I realized that I was actually surrounded by other souls, all as invisible, quiet, and weightless as I. I was totally surrounded by them.

It was black. Quiet. Peaceful. There was no awareness of being contented or discontented. There was no judgment, no conscious thought or understanding other than **"I am. I exist. I have always existed and I will always continue to be in existence."** I understood that our time attached to a physical body is short and has a definite beginning and an end, but our souls will continue forever. With this knowledge, there is no reason to fear death; death has no hold on me.

Recurring Dreams

I understand that many people have recurring dreams that they just can't shake. My recurring dream is that I am not prepared for some major life event, and of course it is my own fault. After self-flagellation and embarrassment, I prepare to be humiliated by others as a result of my ineptness. This dream concept has plagued me for as many years as I can remember.

Often the dream involves me walking into a college classroom to find out that the final exam is today, and I have absolutely no idea what the course is, having never been to class. I didn't even know that I was registered for the class! But I do have a vague recollection of the topic, so maybe I attended for a few weeks? Regardless, I am doomed. Failing this course will mean that I will not be graduating next week, my angry family with non-refundable plane tickets will have no reason to fly out for graduation, my plans to move across the country to start a new job shortly thereafter are moot. My name with my family and in the professional community is ruined, and it is all my fault.

I then experience a sickening feeling of doom in the pit of my stomach. Cue the onslaught of self-talk: Why am I so stupid? Why can't I ever get it right? Why do I continue to be so inept? I don't deserve to be taking up the air that I am breathing. This all results in a full-on assault to my third chakra, my center of self-esteem.

In real life, I wake up exhausted, despising myself, and wonder what am I unprepared for? It takes several minutes to shake the self-hate and despair.

I awoke from one of those dreams just recently. This time, still full of self-flagellation, I entered Open Clinic, and started saying my good mornings to my guides behind me: Divine Mother, Reiki, Christ-Force, Man of God, Archangel Raphael. Before I could move on to Archangel Gabriel, I was firmly tucked under Archangel Raphael's wing and we were off for a lesson. I don't know what he intended to show me, but I intervened and asked if he could please show me why I keep having this recurring dream.

We flew through blue skies and I saw we were headed to a yellow-orange colored energy. We got closer and closer to this energy... the closer we got to the energy, I felt it triggering my second and third chakras, the centers of my emotions, creativity, and sense of self esteem. I recognized the yellow-orange as the same color that my soul was while waiting in the darkness to be incarnated into a body; that moment of "I Am." As soon as I made that mental connection, the atmosphere around me turned black and the yellow-orange energy source pulled further and further away in front of me, falling into the darkness, leaving me and Archangel Raphael in total blackness.

I read somewhere that each of us will have a recurring theme, by which we are driven, life after life. Sounds too simple, but is there a chance that my theme has to do with my second and third chakras, relating to feelings, creativity, and my sense of self? Is that why my soul in the darkness was a pinpoint of yellow-orange?

I had witnessed other souls waiting out there in the darkness, waiting to be incarnated. Were their "I Am" pinpoints robed in the same color as mine or were there pinpoints of different chakra colors signifying the learnings that awaited each soul?

This Soul's Purpose

Another morning in Open Clinic, I watched as I entered Open Clinic dressed in my minister's robe. I started disrobing… black robe, clothes, and all. What in the world was going on? I heard, "Just trust and watch…"

Once again, I watched as I headed back in time to when I was a baby and then before, to the moment my soul was created. In the pitch darkness, I saw my soul as a yellow-orange nugget at the Threshold or the "I Am."

I asked why I was seeing this again. I waited and watched.

I heard the words, "Healer… Teacher… Person of God."

Ah! Thank you! I had just been told my soul's purpose! I had been seeking confirmation, and there it was! My fellow student Caroline's comment ran through my thoughts, "Do you even know how religious you are?"

To the depth of that which formed my soul and my purpose, yes, I believe I do!

CHAPTER 14

The Ministry on Earth

YOUR MONEY'S NO GOOD HERE

I have been asked several times why I don't have an office or accept money in trade for chakra healing, house or business clearings, readings, or Reiki treatments. I have asked my guides that same question. I am not averse to people paying for a clinician's time, so it was not a question of whether I was comfortable with spiritual services for pay. The few times I seriously considered it, I could not come up with a price. My brain would go blank. Not only that, I kept being told, "Not now. You are to work on other things." So, for now, my ministry is not one-on-one readings or clearing energy. While I enjoy doing those things for my friends, it is never with payment in mind.

Trust in the Shadows

This past summer I was feeling particularly vulnerable about the direction my life was heading. I had been spending a great deal of time in meditation, using my intuition, and writing about my experiences. Was I just wasting my time? I went for an early morning walk on the deserted beach to sort out my feelings.

I sat and felt the presence of my spirit guides near me. I asked for validation, some sign that I was indeed on the right track. I asked for evidence that my experiences were valid. Had I really seen angels? What proof could I ask for? More importantly, how could I have come this far and still be questioning all that I have witnessed?

Looking down at the sand and water, I saw a shadow move gracefully across the sand. I looked upward to see what was casting the shadow and saw a seagull high above me. Who knew that a bird that high up could cast such a large shadow on the ground? How had I been to the beach so many times and never seen a gull's shadow before?

Then I understood. Just as the seagull above me could cast a large shadow, angels who were invisible to the naked eye could cast a shadow that is felt energetically during quiet meditation. When I sense the shadow, I can trust that angels are overhead. I can trust that my experiences in the physical and spiritual realms are equally real and equally valid.

As I continued to enjoy the shadows cast by the occasional seagull here or there, I asked for validation that I was on the right track in putting together a book of my experiences. Within a few minutes, I heard a number of gulls approaching. I looked up and counted twenty-one sea gulls approaching me overhead. I smiled at my personal gift of validation.

When I got back to the house, I was curious about the number twenty-one. Why had I seen twenty-one gulls as my message of validation? For grins, I looked up the spiritual meaning of the number twenty-one on SacredScribesAngelNumbers.blogspot.com I read: "The number 21 suggests that there may be some new opportunities or directions for you to take that will lead you in new and exciting directions. Trust that your angels are by your side throughout these changes and transitions and are guiding your every step. They encourage you to remain calm, balanced and happy and you will find that all will work out for your highest good." Wow, thank you!

Joy Comes with the Morning

Back from our beach vacation, I resumed my daily activities. While my daughters were in school, I faithfully wrote my spiritual experiences. I sat down to write and, as usual, grounded my energy, and then asked my guides to join me. I wanted to make sure that what I put in writing was inspired by them and not just my own rambling.

But this day was a little different. I gathered my laptop, papers, and favorite pen from my office and headed to the dining room so I could spread out and write in the same room alongside my Betta fish, Joy. When I found Joy that morning he looked horrible. He was lying on his side on the bottom of his tank, barely breathing.

Joy joined our family last Easter. His colors were Easter pastels and he was so full of life that I just had to bring him home. Every morning when I approached Joy's tank and turned on the lights, he came straight up front to say hello, show off his feathery Betta tail and get breakfast. I noticed that Joy was particularly active when I stopped to chat with him, more so than when other family members fed him. I believe that he recognized me and knew that I could understand him. Joy has certainly lived up to his name!

But this morning, it was obvious that Joy was very sick and probably not going to be with us for long. I pulled Joy's tank close to the edge of the table. I thought if I was going to be surrounded by my healing guides, then Joy should be as well. Noel, the Betta in the neighboring tank, stayed in the closest corner of his tank, keeping watch on Joy.

My dining room had energetically been transposed to a room of service, ministry, and healing. I asked Reiki to send love and healing to Joy's beautiful little spirit. Several times when I glanced over, I saw that Joy's tank had two healing spirits in front of it but I did not recognize either one. Healing at this point could be a miracle to his physical body, or supporting him as he transitioned on.

I started to write. I got distracted by the dryer in the laundry room. I usually work where I won't be disturbed, but this day that was not the case. As I walked across the house to the laundry room, I caught a glimpse in my mind's eye of the color black billowing around my legs. What? I stopped and saw myself energetically. I was wearing my minister's robe! It had never dawned on me that while I was writing these vignettes on behalf of the spirit realm, I was doing so in my role as minister.

I quickly finished the laundry and resumed writing, very mindful of myself as author in a minister's robe. I see the ministry, my ministry, serving a purpose in the spiritual realm and now also in the earthly realm, as I am preparing for others to read my stories.

I checked on Joy several times after the healing visitation. His color was sickly and he mostly rested on the bottom of the tank. Each time he saw me, he took a quick trip up to the top of the tank and floated weakly back down again. His ability to stay upright became less and less, and he rested on his side breathing heavily.

Joy passed during the night. Thank you, Joy, for your enthusiastic love and for sharing your sweet spirit so freely with me.

The Angel

I showed up at Open Clinic and Archangel Michael flew me off on a journey. We ended up in a field. I was told to lie down. I wondered why, but I trusted Archangel Michael, so I did as he requested. I watched as I was transformed into an angel. I looked like me, but with a white gown and white feathery wings! I stood up.

I heard the words, "You are an angel on earth."

Thank you for the beautiful reminder that all light workers and people who choose to spread love and light are serving as angels on earth. Thank you.

THE TRIBUNAL

I walked into Open Clinic one night and I saw the back of a person in a judge's black robe. I turned and left Open Clinic. Why did I leave? I felt like I had been spun out. It felt like a very important conversation was taking place there, and I was not to be participating.

A little later, I fell asleep. I woke in the middle of the night, feeling like I was suffocating energetically. I could not take a deep breath. I asked my guides for a healing. I watched as a long, thick, black, serpent-like creature was being unwrapped from around my throat. The serpent signified fear in my communication space and was keeping me from speaking my truth. But I was not sure about what.

The next morning, I went back into Open Clinic. I saw several entities in judge's robes having a conversation. I was spun out again. Who are these judges and why are they kicking me out of my space? I pushed my way back in. Then I felt their judgment. I heard the following: "How can this be? This is ridiculous; this can't work! This is just wrong!" I felt the condemnation.

Are these judges an outside force? Do they have any power to shut down Open Clinic?

I saw padlocks on the gates. I was frightened. Who has this power to padlock the gates?

I stood in the middle of Open Clinic and asked my guides to join me. They had been relegated up against the back wall. Why? Are these judges more powerful than my guides? I became angry. I would show them what happens here. Then they would see it is legitimate.

I channeled God's love down through my arms for the judges to see. How could they be more powerful than God's love? I saw waves of children's souls come in to receive healing. I tried to read where they were from. My intuitive abilities were blocked, but I heard the word "Serbia." Were they refugees from Serbia? How could my abilities to read energy be blocked? I feared I was no longer in a position of control. The first group of children received healing and left. As they left, another wave of children entered and received healing.

Then it hit me. Are these judges of my own making? I had given four of my friends my One Love manuscript and secretly feared their judgment. Maybe this was them in spirit, checking out all that I had written about? Maybe I was so worried about their skepticism that I allowed the perceived judgments of others to silence Open Clinic. I know that the perceived judgments of others can be damning and have a great deal of power. Would I really allow the judgment of others to censor Open Clinic?

I realized that I had the power to censor Open Clinic if I let my fear of other people's judgment silence me, similar to the serpent in my communication space. I realized that I could never let that happen. The work here is too important.

I stewed over this for a day. Then I thought maybe I had it wrong. Were the judges like-minded to myself and wanted to open clinics of their own? Maybe they were there asking questions about how to replicate it?

Hmm... now that I think about it, who opened Open Clinic in the first place and let me attend? Could whoever opened it also shut it down? Maybe these judges were the ones who opened it and now they were not pleased with my work. Could they take away my gift of ministry? I was anxious and becoming agitated.

I went back to Open Clinic. I looked at those locks on the gates... Wait a minute. One of the things that makes this an open clinic is that it is always open. There are no gates! If there are no padlocks on gates, then maybe there are no judges either! With that realization, I felt a shift in the energy around me.

I entered Open Clinic and saw myself sitting there, curled up, holding my knees. I looked as vulnerable as a person could. I heard an angel start to sing. It was a beautiful, lyrical female voice. I thought of Vivaldi, but without vibrato. Even better.

I got a glimpse of the judge that had its back to the front of Open Clinic. I saw that the judge was not a judge at all. It was Mi, my higher self, sitting there, wearing my black ministerial robe, which happened to look like a judge's robe. The judge, as it turns out, was not judging. She was sitting down to explain Open Clinic to others. Who were the others? My friends who have the manuscript? No. I understood Mi was explaining Open Clinic to the individuals who would be carrying this manuscript forward to make sure that it was published and got into the hands of the people who needed to read it.

OPEN CLINIC FRANCHISES

Is there a way for others to re-create or experience Open Clinic? I don't know, in the same way that I don't know how to bring down healing energy from Mount Chakra. I don't have it figured out... yet. I suppose if I spent enough time studying science, crystals, energetic frequencies, and trans-medium communication I might be able to figure it out.

I am not special. I don't think I have any abilities that other intuitives don't possess. I don't know how I was the one that had access to Open Clinic. It just happened. It was as if the universe threw a ball and I was the one who caught it. Does that mean this was the only Open Clinic "ball" that the universe had? Has the ball been thrown several times before and no one was there, willing or able to catch it? Or conversely, has someone else already been living with an Open Clinic situation and I am just not aware of it? I hope that is the case. Maybe that is the next chapter of my journey: figuring out how I received Open Clinic and figuring out how to help other healers receive access to their own.

In quiet meditation, I saw the walls of Open Clinic being thrust wide open to expand the number of souls that could be impacted by the learning and healing there. I saw the profound abilities of all the healing guides; I felt like I could do anything with them behind me. I knew that I could cast huge amounts of white golden light as a conduit for God. I looked down and my robe had turned to gold.

Ego aside, I know that Open Clinic is bigger than I am. It existed before me and will continue to exist after my time there is complete. I did nothing to deserve it or earn it. I am profoundly fortunate to have been a small part of Open Clinic's existence. And I am profoundly grateful.

THE ASCENSION

For two painful weeks I felt like I was slogging through mud. Everything I touched took too long to complete, or was left undone; the computer had glitches; and appointments got rescheduled. People in my inner circle were frustrated by various disappointments and were dis-regulated due to the changing seasons. Their angst further fueled my discomfort.

I looked out my second floor office window. I saw large crows floating and soaring weightlessly in the autumn breeze. My spirit wanted to soar but my feet were bogged down in the mud. I became frustrated and sullen.

After much soul searching, I finally figured out my cause of distress. I couldn't live with the disconnect between my body on this earth and my spirit in another realm. I couldn't make it make sense and I couldn't hold everything together. I wanted to run away and be by myself so I could choose one realm or the other and not feel so conflicted.

My sister gave me the perfect opportunity to head out of town and I chose to join her. In preparation, I looked for workshops I could download and listen to on the plane. I saw one workshop called The Ascension from the Third Dimension to Fifth Dimension. I remembered reading something about that: people on spiritual journeys learning a great deal about the spiritual realm were sometimes infused with so much healing energy that they were drawn to be more and more spiritual. As a result, they ascended spiritually to a higher realm. Their bodies remained in the physical, the third dimension, in charge of the logistics of daily life. But concurrently, on the spiritual realm, they soared to the fifth dimension and spent time with the angels, Divinity and healers. I wondered if I was ascending and feeling caught between the two dimensions. That would explain my feeling physically trapped while spiritually soaring.

I hoped listening to this workshop could answer my questions and address my discomfort. I put my headphones on before the plane departed. I was in such need of healing that I could not wait. At 33,000 feet, I heard how other intuitives were struggling in the same way that I was. Struggling with Ascension was not a new phenomenon and it was not mine alone. It was a comfort to hear that others had struggled with the exact same dilemmas including disrupted sleep, altered dietary interests, muddled thinking, and desiring to keep one's head in the clouds rather than in one's physical body. Just hearing that others had the same issues provided a level of healing. Guided imagery and meditation then gave me additional healing. By the end of the workshop I was finally at peace and comfortable in my body. By the time I returned to my family a few days later, I was eager to see them and looking forward to spending time together.

I went to clairvoyant class the following week and my colleagues did a reading and energetic healing for me. By reading my energy, they saw that I had been conflicted between the ease in the spirit realm versus my lack of ease in the physical realm. They saw that I was quite comfortable in the spiritual realm and that at times I longed to stay there. They also saw my love for my family and the incongruence of wanting to be functional in both the physical and ethereal realms at once. Delphine said that my experiences looked energetically similar to a near death experience; I loved what I saw in the spiritual realm and struggled when I got called back into my body on earth. Thankfully they offered healing and support.

You Did It!

I walked into Open Clinic and said my good mornings to my guides. They led me to a table and told me to have a seat. Funny, I didn't recall seeing furniture in Open Clinic. Once I was seated, they gathered behind me. I was handed a gold book. I looked closely. One Love was inscribed on the front. I wept with gratitude. I asked what I should do with my book and held it to my heart.

My guides suggested I put it in the new bookshelf behind me. I slid my gold book on the shelf and saw it was next to books written by other authors about Divine Mother and the archangels. I was delighted to see that my book was the only gold one. Thank you for this acknowledgment!

Home at Last

During meditation, I saw myself walk into Oper Clinic. Was I looking at Mi, my higher self? No, it was really me this time. I was wearing a ministerial robe, but it was white! What happened to my black and gold robes? What about my tiles and beads? I cherished them for the learning they represented, as well as for the gifts of love from my guides and Sylvia. I looked down and saw that they were all accounted for and in the exact same location on this robe as on my black robe.

I looked at myself in the white robe. I heard the words "an angel on earth." I remembered the struggle of the Ascension period. I smiled. I am at peace, both in body and in spirit. I am one. I am home.

CHAPTER 15

From the Archangels

I have had truly amazing opportunities to touch the Divine through the archangels, to hear their words, to watch them actively healing souls, and to learn life lessons at their feet. This book has been compiled to share those lessons with other people. Is there a way to let my guides share directly their message with others? Yes, I think so. What if I devoted space to allow each of my guides to share what they wanted people to know?

I sat down with the intention of meeting with each guide one on one. When I approached them, there was general approval for the idea. I soon understood that my personal guides were just that: my personal guides. They had no message for the masses. The archangels and Divine Mother, however, welcomed the opportunity.

Archangel Michael

The one who seemed to be the most excited was Archangel Michael. I had to wait about ten minutes after I thought of the idea before I could sit down and get started. During those ten minutes, there was a great deal of buzzing, frenetic energy around me; it only stopped once I sat down and began listening to Michael.

He showed me his wings; they were huge, twice the size they normally were. I saw the detail of each feather, the large as well as the small in front of me; then the entire wing. I saw gray, a lot of dark gray.

This is what he said:
Love one another.

He showed me that he sees so much hurt and despair that humans put on each other.

It doesn't need to be that way. The world is a difficult place.

If people knew that they had an angel they could rely on, there would not be so much hate.

Hate is people's fear that they are alone. But they don't have to be alone.

Look outside of yourself. Look to a spiritual entity outside of you. God created us so you never need to be alone. We are here to be with you.

Keep us busy.

Don't limit my abilities, my power, by what you think I am capable of doing. If you don't call on me, then you will never know what I can do.

There are a multitude of angels waiting to love you, waiting to help. You don't have to rely on yourself.

Teach your children to look for angels. There are angels that work specifically with children. They are smaller in stature so as not to scare them.

If your child is afraid, you might ask for angels to fill the room, to calm and protect.

Ask for an angel sprite to watch over your baby, to love it, and amuse it.

Ask for an angel to sit with the elderly while they are feeling alone in their apartment or nursing home.

There are enough angels to go around.

Archangel Raphael

I saw a dark brown color the whole time I was hearing from Archangel Raphael.

He said:
The heart.
Let all your dealings be made through your heart. Every conversation with others, speak from your heart.

Live through your heart.

Live your life as if your heart is the captain making your decisions for you.

Your heart is the captain, your soul is the compass, your soul's purpose is your map.

Let others be the beneficiaries of your benevolence.

Archangel Gabriel

I saw a vibrant orange-red with a splash of pink while Gabriel was talking.

She said:
If an idea comes to you, act on it. Write it down. If you don't, you will need to remember it, or it will be gone. Once you have acted on the first thought, another thought will come. Act on it. Write it down.

And then another will come and then another. An inability to act on the first thought stops further thoughts from coming in.

Trust in your ability to create. Create for the world to see you. Not for payment, not for the approval of others, but so the world can see you.

Be creative using vibrant, joyful life.
Feel and love deeply.
Live in color.
Live through color.
Be brave and find your voice.
Sing with all your glory.
Don't just feel passionately, but exude passion.
Let your passion push yourself to the edge, which then gives you a new edge to push toward.

You are the only one who can do what you do, so do it.

Look around you and be inspired by the colors, not once, but many times a day. There is healing in the leaves, the grasses, and the waters of the ocean. Inhale the color; let it flow through you. Exhale to renew the flow and send it positively out to the world so others can heal.

Share your gifts with others as your soul would have you do.

Healing exists in the colors of music.

Divine Mother

Divine Mother showed me pictures as she was talking. She started by showing me a glimpse of my good friend, Denice.

Friendship... that one friend you can count on to let you be you, to share yourself and laugh with. That one friend that makes you feel you are home. That is love.

Find that friendship, that love, in the beauty that surrounds you.
> *In the purple flowers in the field,*
> *in the gold wheat that shimmers*
> *in the sun light,*
> *and the dew on the new,*
> *light green grass in the spring.*

Find that friendship in nature while you are walking in the field at night, in the light of the moon. See the stars. Feel the cool crunch of the plants underfoot. See a field mouse skitter by your foot.

We all belong on this planet together: nature, earth, moon, sun.
Find love in your heart to care for nature.
Find love and joy in each other.

Envelop yourself in peace and calm in your heart.
Exhale.
Love Christ. Love God.
The most important thing in your life is the love of God.

God shows himself in the greens in the grass,
*   the gold of the hay,*
*   in the innocence of animals,*
*   the mystery of night.*

Love God, for in the end, that is all that matters.
All loving. All love.
All encompassing.
All love. All love. God.

From behind, I saw her stretch out her arms in reverence to God.

White light.
White healing light.
White golden healing light.
Purity of all love.
The songs of the angels

I could hear angels singing.

After life, all are at one with the angels.
Chorus of beings.
Hallelujah.
Joy. White light.
Freedom in exulted joy.
Freedom of the soul in exulted joy.

Methodist, Baptist, Catholic, non-denominational.
It doesn't matter.

God is one.
God is love.
One Love. One Love.

About the Author

Dr. Ruth Anderson is a lifelong student and teacher. Retired after a satisfying and worthwhile career in special education and public school administration, Ruth embraced her second calling, that of an intuitive reader and healer. After becoming a Reverend of the Church of Inner Light, she was given a ministry to provide healing to spirits with and without bodies in the ethereal realm called Open Clinic. In Open Clinic, she uses her intuition and God's healing energy, and is assisted by her healing guides, Reiki and Divine Mother, along with archangels Michael, Gabrielle, and Raphael. These experiences make her uniquely qualified to write about Open Clinic. Ruth lives in Colorado and continues to study energetic healing methods.

Ruth's writings can be found at www.theministryonline.org and she can be contacted at openclinic1@outlook.com.